ROBERT F. KENNEDY HUMAN RIGHTS

SPEAK TRUTH TO POWER

A GUIDE TO DEFENDING HUMAN RIGHTS

KERRY KENNEDY

FOR DIGNA OCHOA, AND FOR ALL THOSE
WHO HAVE GIVEN THEIR LIVES TO SECURE BASIC RIGHTS,
AND ALL THE UNSUNG WHO SHOW US
NOT HOW TO BE SAINTS, BUT HOW TO BE FULLY HUMAN;
FOR MY DAUGHTERS, CARA, MARIAH, AND MICHAELA—AND
FOR ALL CHILDREN.
KERRY KENNEDY

CONTENTS

- **4** INTRODUCTION
- **6** FOREWORD BY KERRY KENNEDY
- **8** DEFENDER MAP

DEFENDER INTERVIEWS:

- **10** **FRANK MUGISHA**
  Uganda
- **14** **RANA HUSSEINI**
  Jordan
- **18** **MUHAMMAD YUNUS**
  Bangladesh
- **22** **MARIAN WRIGHT EDELMAN**
  United Sates
- **26** **WANGARI MAATHAI**
  Kenya
- **32** **KAILASH SATYARTHI**
  India

ELEMENTARY:

- **38** WHAT ARE HUMAN RIGHTS?
- **40** ADAPTING LESSONS FOR ANY GRADE LEVEL
- **42** **LOUNE VIAUD**
  Haiti, Needs and Wants
- **46** **LUCAS BENITEZ**
  United States, Right to Work
- **52** ACTIVITIES FOR THOUGHTFUL REFLECTION
- **54** UNIVERSAL DECLARATION OF HUMAN RIGHTS
  Simplified Version

MIDDLE SCHOOL:

- **58** **MALALA YOUSAFZAI**
  Pakistan, Right to Education
- **66** **JAMIE NABOZNY**
  United States, Anti-Bullying
- **76** **DESMOND TUTU**
  South Africa, Reconciliation

HIGH SCHOOL:

- **86** **ROBERT F. KENNEDY**
  United States, Justice
- **94** **RIGOBERTA MENCHÚ TUM**
  Guatemala, Indigenous People's Rights
- **102** **VAN JONES**
  United States, Law Enforcement

UNIVERSITY:

- **112** **MARINA PISKLAKOVA**
  Russia, Domestic Violence
- **120** **THE DALAI LAMA**
  Tibet, Religious Freedom
- **130** **JULIANA DOGBADZI**
  Ghana, Slavery and Trafficking
- **138** SPEAK TRUTH TO POWER
  Voices From Beyond The Dark
- **142** ACKNOWLEDGEMENTS

ROBERT F. KENNEDY HUMAN RIGHTS

Speak Truth To Power:
THE PROGRAM

Robert F. Kennedy Human Rights' Speak Truth To Power (STTP) program evolved from Kerry Kennedy's book, *Speak Truth To Power: Human Rights Defenders Who Are Changing Our World,* first printed in English in 2000, and has since been printed in seven languages. Featuring interviews with more than 50 human rights defenders, including Nobel Peace Prize winners Wangari Maathai, Archbishop Desmond Tutu, Elie Wiesel and Muhammad Yunus, the book is a remarkable tribute to the indomitable human spirit. Endorsing this book, Nelson Mandela wrote, "The lives of common women and men, in this book, heroes every one, inspire all who believe in liberty and justice."

Alongside the interviews, in the original book, are portraits by Pulitzer Prize-winning photographer Eddie Adams, which have since been developed into a museum-quality exhibition. The exhibition began its international tour at The Corcoran Gallery, Washington, D.C. and has since traveled to four continents, reaching countries such as Cambodia, Greece, Italy, Qatar, Slovakia, Spain, Sweden, South Korea and South Africa. Most recently it was displayed at Baltimore-Washington Thurgood Marshall International Airport for six months, major train stations throughout Sweden, and in public spaces throughout Norway.

Award-winning playwright Ariel Dorfman adapted the words from the book into a play, *Speak Truth To Power: Voices From Beyond the Dark.* Hosted by President Bill Clinton, the play premiered at the Kennedy Center in 2000. A one-hour video was broadcast on PBS as part of its Great Performances Series. Many of our greatest actors have performed in the play, including Alec Baldwin, Glenn Close, John Malkovich, Sean Penn, Vanessa Redgrave, Martin Sheen, and Meryl Streep. The play has been produced across the United States and performed by major actors in capitals around the world. Notably, a performance in Doha, Qatar, was transmitted live on the Arab news network Al Jazeera and read by ten of the most celebrated actors and singers of the Arab world. It has also been performed by school children, college students, local heroes, and even prisoners. In 2014, at the European Union in Brussels, several Members of the European Parliament, including Martin Schulz, President of the European Parliament, performed the play.

The Speak Truth To Power human rights education curriculum, comprised of over fifty lesson plans, has been taught to millions of students from kindergarten through law school in Africa, Asia, Europe, North America, and South America. As an educational tool for students at every grade level, the curriculum shows students that they, too, can make a difference in the global struggle for justice. STTP uses the stories of courageous heroes from around the world to teach students about human rights and empower them to become defenders themselves. As students begin to self-identify as human rights defenders, they learn to take active roles in the work of creating a more just and peaceful world. What sets Speak Truth To Power apart is its power to inspire action. By allowing students to see themselves as human rights defenders, they begin to act as human rights defenders.

In addition to the curriculum and the play, the Speak Truth To Power project includes a video contest, a partnership with the American Federation of Teachers (AFT) and the Tribeca Film Institute (TFI) and a music contest, a partnership with the GRAMMY Museum. Both contests are aimed at encouraging students to create change through film and music.

This 2016 edition of the *Speak Truth To Power* book contains six searing and uplifting defender interviews (four of which are included in the first edition) that examine the meaning of courage with men and women who have dramatically changed, and continue to influence, the course of events in their communities and countries. Also included in this book are elementary, middle school, high school and university lesson plans from the Speak Truth To Power curriculum, which give an overview of human rights and social justice issues in the United States and around the world. The toolkit for action gives students and the broader public the resources needed to address issues at local, national, and global levels.

Speak Truth To Power encourages governments, NGOs, major foundations, and individuals to support human rights, and brings much-needed attention to continuing abuses. But perhaps its most lasting effect will be to demonstrate the capacity of each individual to create change.

Visit www.rfkhumanrights.org for more information about Speak Truth To Power, including the full curricula, the play, and how to display the photo exhibit; www.speakupsingout.org to learn more about our music contest and www.speaktruthvideo.com to learn more about our video contest.

FOREWORD
by Kerry Kennedy

In a world when a common lament is that there are no more heroes, too often cynicism and despair are perceived as evidence of the death of moral courage. That perception is wrong. People of great valor and heart, committed to a noble purpose, with long records of personal sacrifice, walk among us in every country of the world. Nearly twenty years ago, I traveled the globe to forty countries and five continents, interviewing individuals who appear in the pages of the first edition of *Speak Truth To Power*, and in the Ariel Dorfman play. These are people whose lives are filled with extraordinary feats of bravery. I've listened to them speak about the quality and nature of courage, and in their stories I found hope and inspiration, a vision of a better world.

For many of these heroes, their understanding of the abrogation of human rights has been profoundly shaped by their personal experiences: of death threats, imprisonment, and in some cases, bodily harm. However, this is not, by any measure, a compilation of victims. Rather, courage, with its affirmation of possibility and change, is what defines them, singly and together. Each spoke with compelling eloquence of the causes to which they have devoted their lives, and for which they are willing to sacrifice—from freedom of expression to the rule of law, from environmental defense to the eradication of bonded labor, from access to capital to the right to due process, from women's rights to religious liberty. These leaders hold in common an inspiring record of accomplishment and a profound capacity to ignite change.

The defenders' own voices provoke fundamental questions: why do people who face imprisonment, torture, and death, continue to pursue their work when the chance of success is so remote and the personal consequences are so grave? Why did they become involved? What keeps them going? Where do they derive their strength and inspiration? How do they overcome their fear? How do they measure success? Out of their answers emerges a sympathetic and strength-giving portrait of the power of personal resolve and determination in the face of injustice. These fundamental questions have a special interest for me personally. As a mother of three girls, I deeply wished to understand if there were steps I could take to encourage my own daughters to develop similar attributes, or if moral courage was something certain people are born with, inherently, while the rest of us (with our own lesser sensibilities) are left to muddle through. And if we are capable of less, then are we off the hook? Condemned to be sinners, is there any point in striving to be saints?

Several defenders recalled an early moment or incident that galvanized their social conscience forever. Some told stories of searing childhood encounters with injustice. Many defenders are members of groups that have endured sustained repression, and so have come to a natural understanding of the issues and desire to overcome the wrongs, like former sexual slave Juliana Dogbadzi, whose story is told in one of the university lesson plans. Others saw injustice in a community they were not a part of and took up the cause. And still others had enjoyed the comforts of being among the elite in their countries, yet risked banishment—and worse—to right wrongs committed by their peers.

Despite the overwhelming powers arrayed against them, these men and women are, as a whole, an optimistic lot. In my interview with Archbishop Tutu, he emphasized this attitude, saying, "We have a God who doesn't say, 'Ah... Got you!' No. God says, 'Get up,' and God dusts us off and God says, 'Try again.'" Perhaps the stance should be qualified as less optimistic than hopeful. Overwhelmingly pragmatic and realistic about the prospects for change, all too aware of the challenges they face, nonetheless they continue to roll their boulders back up the hill.

These voices are, most of all, a call to action, much needed because human rights violations often occur by cover of dark, in remote places. For many of those who suffer, isolation is their worst enemy, and exposure of the atrocities is their only hope. We must bring the international spotlight to violations and broaden the community of those who know and care about the individuals portrayed. This alone may well stop a disappearance, cancel a torture session, or even, save a life.

I grew up in the Judeo-Christian tradition where our prophets were painted on ceilings and our saints were sealed in stained glass. They were superhuman, untouchable, and so we were freed from the burden of their challenge. But here on Earth, people like these and countless other defenders are living, breathing human beings in our midst. Their determination, valor, and commitment in the face of overwhelming danger challenge each of us to take up the torch for a more decent society. Today we are blessed by the presence of these people. They are teachers who show us not how to be saints, but how to be fully human.

In these pages you will find both the stories of the most courageous people on Earth, and ways in which educators from kindergarten through university can bring those stories to life in the classroom and beyond.

Robert F. Kennedy once called education, "the key to human dignity"—the key to a more just and peaceful world.

> "IN A WORLD WHEN A COMMON LAMENT IS THAT THERE ARE NO MORE HEROES, TOO OFTEN CYNICISM AND DESPAIR ARE PERCEIVED AS EVIDENCE OF THE DEATH OF MORAL COURAGE. THAT PERCEPTION IS WRONG. PEOPLE OF GREAT VALOR AND HEART, COMMITTED TO A NOBLE PURPOSE, WITH LONG RECORDS OF PERSONAL SACRIFICE, WALK AMONG US IN EVERY COUNTRY OF THE WORLD."—Kerry Kennedy

1 **FRANK MUGISHA** Uganda
2 **RANA HUSSEINI** Jordan
3 **MUHAMMAD YUNUS** Bangladesh
4 **MARIAN WRIGHT EDELMAN** United Sates
5 **WANGARI MAATHAI** Kenya
6 **KAILASH SATYARTHI** India
7 **LOUNE VIAUD** Haiti
8 **LUCAS BENITEZ** United States
9 **MALALA YOUSAFZAI** Pakistan
10 **JAMIE NABOZNY** United States
11 **DESMOND TUTU** South Africa
12 **ROBERT F. KENNEDY** United States
13 **RIGOBERTA MENCHÚ TUM** Guatemala
14 **VAN JONES** United States
15 **MARINA PISKLAKOVA** Russia
16 **THE DALAI LAMA** Tibet
17 **JULIANA DOGBADZI** Ghana

FRANK MUGISHA
Uganda—LGBT Rights

In Uganda, a country of 33 million people, Frank Mugisha advocates against legislation or other governmental crackdowns on LGBT people in Uganda. In 2007, Mr. Mugisha was chosen to lead Sexual Minorities Uganda (SMUG), a coalition of LGBT human rights organizations. As a result of his public advocacy, Mr. Mugisha has lost jobs, friends and has become estranged from members of his family. A close colleague at SMUG, David Kato, was brutally murdered in his home after being outed in a local newspaper. Undeterred by threats of violence, Frank Mugisha continues to amplify the aspirations of Uganda's most vulnerable communities. In 2011, Frank Mugisha received the Robert F. Kennedy Human Rights Award.

INTERVIEW BY KERRY KENNEDY, 2011

> "BECOMING AN ACTIVIST WAS A GRADUAL PROCESS FOR ME. EVERY TIME I MET A UGANDAN PERSON AND WAS ABLE TO CHANGE HIS MIND ABOUT HOMOSEXUALITY, IT MADE ME WANT TO CONTINUE. I HAVE TO WORK VERY HARD AND SPEAK OUT TO MAKE A CHANGE. MAYBE OUT OF 33 MILLION UGANDANS I CAN REACH SEVEN. MAYBE AT SOME POINT I CAN REACH 15 MILLION. AND MAYBE YEARS TO COME, SOMEONE WILL PICK UP FROM WHERE I LEFT OFF." –Frank Mugisha

I was six or seven years old when I realized I was attracted to people of my own sex. I thought I was alone. There were all sorts of bad names for homosexuals. But the way people talked wasn't relating to who I was. I am a good person. I could not tell anyone for the fear that I would get all the bad names. As my understanding grew, I would see people expelled from school for rumors of being homosexuals. When the expelled students went home, their fathers threatened to kill them, or their families threw them out of the house. Sometimes the expelled student would be sent to live with grandparents in the village and do farming. His education ended. My fear increased.

I had so many dreams. I wanted to be a doctor or a lawyer. If I got kicked out of school, I could never become a lawyer or a doctor. I decided that I would never tell anyone. So I tried to fit in and be like my other colleagues. I tried to change myself. I would pray to God. It wasn't working. At 14, I decided to tell someone because I couldn't keep it in anymore. I only told friends who were very close to me, but I lost very many friends. And the rumor was spread in school that I was a homosexual. The disciplinary committee asked me if I was a homosexual. I couldn't say yes or no. I just went quiet and cried. So they told me to bring my parent.

I didn't tell my mother that I was a homosexual. I told her that the school thinks I am a homosexual. She didn't ask me anything. She came to school, and I was excused from the meeting. When they called me back into the meeting, the school said that my discipline track record was the best. I was also a prefect so I was excused. I felt good about it. Now they know and they didn't expel me. So I can still go on and tell people. I told my brother, and he just laughed about it. And for me that was good. But he didn't keep quiet. He started telling everyone.

A year later my mother took me to talk to a religious leader in Uganda, and he started quoting verses in the bible. The things he was telling me, strange things, were not relating to me at all. I wanted someone to tell me something that relates to what I am feeling inside. I told my mom that I wish I was made out of bricks because bricks are there, and no one hurts them—bricks just build houses. Why didn't God create me into something that is never harassed? Why do I have to endure all this? I believe in God. I can recite the rosary from my head. I am not being rebellious or committing sins. This is happening to me because I have no control over it.

That is the reason I tried so hard to change myself. Because I believed homosexuality could be a sin. A friend said that I was going to go to hell. And I thought to myself, what should I do to change this?

When I started understanding that I cannot change myself and that I loved my religion, I decided not to listen to people. What they were telling me wasn't what I felt inside. At some point I thought that maybe prayer was affecting me, so I stopped praying. But it was very difficult to wake up one morning and wash religion out of my head. I am what I am and that's it.

Becoming an activist was a gradual process for me. Every time I met a Ugandan person and was able to change his mind about homosexuality, it made me want to continue. I have to work very hard and speak out to make a change. Maybe out of 33 million Ugandans I can reach seven. Maybe at some point I can reach 15 million. And maybe years to come, someone will pick up from where I left off. But at least I have paved the avenue to understanding.

Just appearing on television in Uganda and speaking out helps many people accept themselves. They know they are not alone in the world. They know there is a voice out there for them. That is where I get my courage: knowing that every day of my life, every minute of my life, I make a very small difference, but that small difference has a huge impact on so many different people.

For activists like myself, the Ugandans are our biggest threats. The moment you come out and say you are gay in Uganda, the discrimination begins. Friends and family reject you. Employers throw you out of your job. You never know who is going to harass you, bully you, attack you in the streets, or even arrest you. I can't go shopping. I don't know if it is safe to use public transportation. Before I leave my house I have to calculate—will I be safe? Should I go anywhere or should I just stay home? Everyday someone will call me to say a friend has been arrested or beaten or thrown out of his house for being gay.

There are many homosexuals who have been arrested in Uganda and tortured while in jail. People have been beaten on the streets. Villagers break into houses of a suspected homosexual and beat the person up or take him to prison and tell the authorities he's a homosexual. Lesbian girls are raped by their own relatives. The family will ask an uncle to rape the girl and teach her to be a woman. The girl will be raped almost every night. And some girls have to leave their families because they can't live there anymore and run away, maybe in the middle of the night, run off to nowhere, to the streets.

There is discrimination when gay men seek out health care services. I lost a friend who was living with HIV. He died in a hospital. But the reason he died was because he was afraid to tell the doctors he was gay. If he told the doctors they would leave him alone and not talk to him. If he told his family, they would not help him. He was in the hospital alone, so I talked to the doctors so they would give him the right medication. But the reaction wasn't good. He was put off the bed to the floor. If it wasn't for the fear and the stigma, he wouldn't have died.

One of the reasons we do activism and create visibility is to try and stop the media from outing people. If the media want our faces, we're here. We'll show our faces and tell you the truth about our sexuality. But stop outing people who are not ready to be out. A tabloid newspaper called Red Pepper started outing people. They named people and included their home addresses and places where they worked. But the worst was a Ugandan tabloid called Rolling Stone which published names and photos with headlines that homosexuals need to be killed. When the article came out, almost everyone who appeared in the paper was harassed. We had to stop it. We asked and begged the media to respect people, but they refused. So we took them to court. Fortunately, the court ruled that publishing the names of people who are perceived to be homosexual is an invasion of privacy. Rolling Stone keeps publishing articles filled with misinformation, but they can't publish names and pictures anymore.

My colleague, David Kato, was murdered after his picture was published in the paper. Murdered in his home in his own bed at night. No one knows who did it or why. I think about it all the time. David once told me that he couldn't live if he wasn't doing activism. I don't know if I would live if I wasn't doing activism. I go through a lot of challenges, and all those images come back to me. I am driven by the images. I am driven by the stories of the people I've met. I want to see change happen within the next few hours.

RANA HUSSEINI
Jordan – Honor Killings

Jordanian journalist Rana Husseini broke a country's silence when she unveiled the crime of honor killing in Jordan. Honor killings happen after women are raped or accused of participating in illicit sexual activity. Such women are considered to have compromised the honor of their family. Fathers, brothers, and sons may see it as their duty to avenge the offense. They do this not by pursuing the perpetrators but by murdering the victims—their own daughters, sisters, or mothers. In 1999 it was estimated that honor killings accounted for one-third of the murders of women in Jordan.

In the 1990s Husseini began writing reports on the killings. As a result, she was threatened and accused of being anti-Islam, anti-family, and anti-Jordan. Yet Husseini soon gained support among Jordan's royal family. Queen Noor—the wife of King Hussein, who reigned during 1953–99—took up the cause. Moreover, in a speech to Jordan's parliament in 1997, King Hussein himself denounced violence against women.

Husseini eventually earned several international awards for her reporting on honor killings. In 2007 King Abdullah II awarded her a medal for her activism. Husseini has continued her work in the firm belief that exposing the truth about violence against women is the first step toward stopping it.

INTERVIEW TAKEN FROM KERRY KENNEDY'S BOOK *SPEAK TRUTH TO POWER*, 2000

"MANY FAMILIES TIE THEIR REPUTATION TO THE WOMEN. IF SHE DOES SOMETHING WRONG, THE ONLY WAY TO RECTIFY THE FAMILY'S HONOR IS TO HAVE A WIFE, DAUGHTER, SISTER KILLED. BLOOD CLEANSES HONOR." –Rana Husseini

I never imagined that I would work on women's issues when, in September 1993, I was assigned as the crime reporter at The Jordan Times. In the beginning I wrote about thefts, accidents, fires—all minor cases. Then, after about four or five months on the job, I started coming across crimes of honor. One story really shocked me and compelled me to get more involved.

In the name of honor, a sixteen-year-old girl was killed by her family because she was raped by her brother. He assaulted her several times and then threatened to kill her if she told anyone. When she discovered that she was pregnant, she had to tell her family. After the family arranged an abortion, they married her off to a man fifty years her senior. When he divorced her six months later, her family murdered her.

An honor killing occurs when a male relative decides to take the life of a female relative because, in his opinion, she has dishonored her family's reputation by engaging in an "immoral" act. An immoral act could be that she was simply seen with a strange man or that she slept with a man. In many cases, women are killed just because of rumors or unfounded suspicions.

When I went to investigate the crime I met with her two uncles. At first, when I questioned them about the murder, they got defensive and asked, "Who told you that?" I said it was in the newspaper. They started telling me that she was "not a good girl." So I asked, "Why was it her fault that she had been raped? Why didn't the family punish her brother?" And they both looked at each other, and one uncle said to the other, "What do you think? Do you think we killed the wrong person?" The other replied, "No, no. Don't worry. She seduced her brother." I asked them why, with millions of men in the street, would she choose to seduce her own brother? They only repeated that she had tarnished the family image by committing an impure act. Then they started asking me questions: "Why was I dressed like this? Why wasn't I married? Why had I studied in the United States?" They inferred that I, too, was not a good girl.

From then on I went on covering stories about women who were killed in an unjust, inhuman way. Most of them did not commit any immoral, much less illegal, act, and even if they did, they still did not deserve to die.

But I want to emphasize two things. One is that all women are not threatened in this way in my country. These crimes are isolated and limited, although they do cross class and education boundaries. The other thing is a lot of people assume incorrectly that these crimes are mandated by Islam, but they are not. Islam is very strict about killing, and in the rare instances where killing is counseled, it is when adultery is committed within a married couple. In these cases, there must be four eyewitnesses, and the punishment must be carried out by the community, not by the family members involved.

Honor killings are part of a culture, not a religion, and occur in Arab communities in the United States and many countries. One-third of the reported homicides in Jordan are honor killings. The killers are treated with leniency. Families assign the task of honor killing to a minor, because under Jordanian juvenile law, minors who commit crimes are sentenced to a juvenile center where they can learn a profession and continue their education, and then, at eighteen, be released without a criminal record. The average term served for an honor killing is only seven and a half months.

The reason for these killings is that many families tie their reputation to the women. If she does something wrong, the only way to rectify the family's honor is to have a wife, daughter, sister killed. Blood cleanses honor. The killers say, "Yes, she's my sister and I love her, but it is a duty."

I undertook this issue not just because I am a woman, but because most people fight for human rights in general—political agendas, prison conditions, children's rights. But nobody is taking up this issue. And isn't it important to guarantee the right of a woman simply to live before fighting for any other laws?

Related to this is the practice of protective custody. If a woman becomes pregnant out of wedlock, she will turn herself in to the police, and they'll put her in prison to "protect her life." Anywhere else in the world you would put the person who is threatening someone's life in prison, but in my country and elsewhere in the Arab world, it is the opposite. The victim goes to jail. Most of these women are held there indefinitely. They are not charged, and they cannot make bail. If the family bails them out, it is to kill them. So these women remain, wasting their lives in prison.

Since I started reporting on the honor killings, things have started to change for the better. When King Hussein opened the Thirteenth Parliament [in 1997], he mentioned women and their rights—the first time a ruler had emphasized women and children. And now King [Abdullah] is following in his father's footsteps, with a new constitution where he put in two new sections, one on women. And he asked the prime minister to amend all the laws that discriminate against women. What was not included was a solution; we could begin with a shelter for women. Instead of putting women who seek haven from their families in prison, the government could have programs to rehabilitate them.

Of course this kind of human rights work has its critics. People have accused me of encouraging adultery and premarital sex. Once I had this man threatening that if I didn't stop writing, he would "visit me" at the newspaper. What upsets me the most is that people want to stay away from the subject by using these excuses. One woman said, "So what if twenty-five women are killed every year; look at how many illegitimate children are born every year?" So sad. People try to divert the main issue by accusing the victim and portraying evil women as the main cause of why adultery takes place. Women are always blamed in my country, and elsewhere in the world.

It is important to realize that people who commit the killings are also victims. Their families put all the burden and pressure on their back. If you don't kill, you are responsible for the family's dishonor. If you do kill, you will be a hero, and everyone will be proud of you.

While I was studying in the United States, I felt that there were good people who were trying to work for other people who were in need of help. I came to believe that if you want to do something or change something, you could do it. But in Jordan many people are passive. They don't care. Many believe that whatever they do will not affect anything in society. But I am convinced this is wrong. Because we can't say, "Okay, I won't do this because nothing will change." If you adopt this attitude, then it's true: nothing will ever change. I hope the day will come when I will no longer need to report on these crimes. This will happen when Jordan modernizes, not only materially, but in its awareness of human rights for women. And I am sure that day will come, and it may be closer than we think.

MUHAMMAD YUNUS
Bangladesh—Microcredit

Founder of the Grameen Bank, the world's largest and most successful microcredit institution, Muhammad Yunus was born in one of the poorest places on earth, the country of Bangladesh (then part of Pakistan). As a professor of economics, he was struck by the discrepancy between the economic theory taught in universities and the abject poverty around him. Recognizing that the poor remained poor because they had no access to capital, no collateral for loans, and borrowing needs so modest that it was not cost-effective for large banks to process their needs, Yunus started experimenting with small, collateral-free loans to landless rural peasants and impoverished women.

In 1983, he founded the Grameen Bank. Its rules were strict and tough. Clients find four friends to borrow with. If any of the five default, all are held accountable, building commitment and providing community support. Initial loans are as small as ten dollars, and must be repaid with 20 percent interest.

Decades later, this revolutionary bank is flourishing, with over eight million customers, nearly all of them women. Ninety-eight percent of Grameen's borrowers repay their loans in full. More importantly, the clients are transforming their lives: from powerless and dependent to self-sufficient, independent, and politically astute. The real transformation will be felt by the next generation, a generation with better food, education, medication, and the firsthand satisfaction of taking control of their lives, thanks to Yunus's vision, creativity, and confidence. In 2006, Yunus and Grameen Bank were awarded the Nobel Peace Prize. In 2013, Yunus was given the Robert F. Kennedy Human Rights Ripple of Hope Award.

INTERVIEW TAKEN FROM KERRY KENNEDY'S BOOK *SPEAK TRUTH TO POWER*, 2000

"WHEN SHE FINISHES HER FIFTIETH INSTALLMENT, THE LAST ONE, AND SHE HAS NOW PAID IN FULL, SHE CAN SAY, 'I DID IT!' IT'S NOT JUST A MONETARY TRANSACTION THAT HAS BEEN COMPLETED; IT IS NOTHING LESS THAN THE TRANSFORMATION OF THAT PERSON. NOW SHE IS A WOMAN WHO FEELS LIKE SHE IS SOMEBODY."–Muhammad Yunus

When I started the Grameen program to provide access to credit for the poor, I came upon two major obstacles. First, commercial banks were institutionally biased against women. Secondly, they had absolutely blocked credit to the poor by demanding something no poor person has access to: namely, collateral.

After overcoming the second issue [by not requiring collateral], I addressed the first. I wanted half of the borrowers from banks in my program to be women. At first, women were reluctant to accept loans. They said, "No, no, I have never touched money in my life. You must go to my husband. He understands money. Give the money to him." My colleagues and I worked hard to come up with a way we could build trust in women so that they would accept loans from men. We slowed down our work just to include more women, since this trust-building took time.

Six years later, proud that half our loans were to women, we began to see something very remarkable. Money that went to families through women helped the families much more than the same amount of money going to men. Unlike men, women were very cautious with money and passed benefits on to their children immediately. They had learned how to manage with scarce resources. And women had a longer vision; they could see a way out of poverty and had the discipline to carry out their plans. Perhaps because women suffer so much more from poverty than men, they are more motivated to escape it.

We decided to make a concerted effort to attract women clients because we got much more mileage out of the same amount of money. It has worked in ways we never anticipated. For instance, women borrowers decided to commit themselves to a set of promises that they called the "sixteen decisions." These are commitments to improve the welfare of the borrowers and their families above and beyond the loans. They agreed to send their children to school, to create unity, to work hard in all their endeavors. They agreed to keep their families small, to plant as many seedlings as possible, even to eat vegetables. These are some of the resolutions created by the women, not imposed by the bank. These aspirations were critical to their lives.

A typical initial loan is something like thirty-five dollars. The night before a woman is going to accept that money from the bank, she will be tossing and turning to decide whether she is really ready for it. She is scared that maybe something terrible will happen to her. And finally in the morning her friends will come over and they will try to persuade her. And finally, with their encouragement, she will come to the bank.

When she holds that money, it is such a huge amount in her hands; it is like holding the hope and treasure that she never dreamt she would achieve. She will tremble, tears will roll down her cheeks, and she won't believe we would trust her with such a large sum. And she promises that she will pay back this money, because the money is the symbol of the trust put in her, and she does not want to betray that trust.

And then she struggles to pay that first loan, that first installment, which is due the following week, and the second installment, which is payable the following week, and this goes on for fifty weeks in sequence, and every time that she repays another installment she is braver! And when she finishes her fiftieth installment, the last one, and she has now paid in full, she can say, "I did it!" It's not just a monetary transaction that has been completed; it is nothing less than a transformation of that person. Now she is a woman who feels like she is somebody. Now she can almost stand up and challenge the whole world, shouting, "I can do it, I can make it on my own."

You see, if you only look at the lending program of Grameen, you have missed most of its impact. Grameen is involved in a process of transformation. The "sixteen decisions" is an example: we found that Grameen children attend school in record numbers because their mothers really take that commitment seriously. And now many of the children are continuing in colleges, universities, going on to medical schools, and so on.

There are other side effects. Starting seven years back we encouraged Grameen borrowers to participate in the political process by voting. Their first reaction was negative. They said, "The candidates are all devils, so why should we vote for them?" It was very depressing that people looked at their electoral process in that way. So we replied, "Okay, yes, they are all devils, but if you don't go and vote, the worst devil will get elected. So go sit down in your centers, discuss who could be the worst, what could happen if he gets elected, and if you find this prospect terrible, then you have an opportunity to choose among all the devils, the least evil." People immediately got excited, and we had almost 100 percent participation in that first election.

Then, in last year's local elections, we were shocked to see that many Grameen members themselves got elected. They said, "You told us to select the least of the devils, and we tried, but it was such an ugly job that we got fed up, and we started looking at each other, thinking, 'Why are we looking for the least devil, when we are good people here? Why don't we run ourselves?'"

Of course there is resistance. The first resistance came from the husbands who felt insulted, humiliated, threatened that their wives were given a loan and they were not. The tension within the family structure sometimes led to violence against the women. So we paused for a while and then came up with an idea. We started meeting with the husbands and explaining the program in a way where they could see it would be beneficial to their family. And we made sure to meet with husbands and wives together so everyone understood what was expected. So that reduced a lot of initial resistance by the husbands.

Neighborhood men also raised objections, and [they] cloaked the fact that they felt threatened by women's empowerment in religious trappings. We carefully examined whether our program was in some way antireligious. But they were hiding behind religion instead of admitting that they felt bypassed. It was the male ego speaking in religious terms.

Our best counterargument was just to give it time. It soon became clear that our borrowers were still attending to their religious duties, at the same time earning money and becoming confident. Women started confronting the religious people. They said, "You think taking money from Grameen Bank is a bad idea? Okay, we won't take any more—if you give the money yourself. We don't care who gives it to us, but without money we cannot do anything." And of course the religious advocates said, "No, no, we can't give you money." So that was the end of that.

We also received criticism from development professionals who insisted that giving tiny loans to women who do not have knowledge and skill does not bring about structural change in the country or the village and therefore is not true development at all. They said development involves multimillion-dollar loans for enormous infrastructure projects. We never expected opposition from the development quarter, but it happened, and became controversial. Because what we do is not in their book. They cannot categorize us, whether right, left, conservative, or liberal. We talk free market, but at the same time we are pro-poor. They are totally confused.

Grameen Bank is now all over Bangladesh. Even in hard times, like this year's terrible flood, people are willingly paying, and we're getting really good loans. That demonstrated the basic ability of the people to do something that they believe in, no matter what others say. People ask, what is the reason that we succeeded, that we could do it, when everybody said it couldn't be done. I keep saying that I was stubborn. So when you ask if it took courage, I would instead say it took stubbornness. No matter what kind of beautiful explanation you give, that's what it takes to make it happen.

MARIAN WRIGHT EDELMAN
United States—Children, Poverty and Racism

Marian Wright Edelman is the founder and President of the Children's Defense Fund (CDF), the foremost children's advocacy organization in the United States. She also is a lawyer, lecturer, civil rights activist, political strategist, and best-selling author. Her courage and action have made her a central figure in the quest for justice for the poor and dispossessed.

Edelman grew up in a closely knit, deeply religious family in a small, racially segregated southern town. She attended Spelman College in Atlanta, Georgia, where she joined civil rights protests. After graduating from Spelman in 1960, she earned a law degree from Yale University in 1963.

Edelman then became the first African American woman qualified to practice law in Mississippi. In the mid-1960s she directed the NAACP Legal Defense and Educational Fund in Jackson, Mississippi. She and her coworkers were regularly harassed, intimidated, and threatened for their civil rights work. In 1968 Edelman was a major force behind the Poor People's March, the last great campaign of Martin Luther King, Jr.

In 1973 Edelman founded CDF. Its mission—"to ensure every child a healthy start, a head start, a fair start, a safe start, and a moral start in life"—reflects her tough-minded idealism. Under Edelman's direction, CDF provides an effective voice for poor and minority children and those with disabilities. It researches and disseminates information on legislation affecting the lives of children. It also provides support to a network of state and local child advocates. A great inspirational leader, Edelman earned the Presidential Medal of Freedom in 2000.

INTERVIEW TAKEN FROM KERRY KENNEDY'S BOOK *SPEAK TRUTH TO POWER*, 2000

"IT IS ABSOLUTELY OBSCENE THAT WE ARE THE SOLE REMAINING SUPERPOWER, NUMBER ONE IN MILITARY EXPENDITURES, FIRST IN HEALTH TECHNOLOGY, FIRST IN BILLIONAIRES AND MILLIONAIRES, [AND] YET WE LET OUR CHILDREN BE THE POOREST GROUP OF AMERICANS."–Marian Wright Edelman

It must be hard to be a poor child in America—hard, when so many have so much, to have little and to know it. When I was growing up in the South, without television, we didn't have the sense that one had to have all these things that our excessively materialistic society tells us we need. People didn't see poverty as something that set them apart. To be poor today, to be unable to get the basic necessities of life, and then to have the judgment about who you are as a person be based on material wealth, is much more difficult. Most of our measures of success have become external.

It is absolutely obscene that we are the sole remaining superpower, number one in military expenditures, first in health technology, first in billionaires and millionaires, [and] yet we let our children be the poorest group of Americans. All the industrialized countries protect their children against preventable diseases and sickness better than we do. We have much higher rates of infant mortality and low-birth-weight babies than our industrialized counterparts. We lag in preparing our children in science, math, and reading. And we lag most shamefully in protecting our children against violence. American children fifteen and under are twelve times more likely to die from gun violence than children in twenty-five other industrialized countries combined.

The fact that we spend more of our resources on military expenditures is not disconnected from the obsession we have with, and the glorification of, violence in our culture. We calculated how many Americans have killed themselves or other people in our own nation between 1968 and 1997. The total is 1.4 million. That is more than all the American battle casualties in all the wars in which we participated in this century. Between 1979 and 1997, nearly 80,000 children were killed by guns, far more than we lost in battle casualties in Vietnam. [T]his slaughter, the presence of guns, and the worship and tolerance of violence as power is something we are going to have to confront.

As a nation, we've got the means to prevent child gun deaths and to end child poverty and preventable diseases, but we haven't got the will. Here we have poverty killing children, more slowly but just as surely as guns. So I hope that we will find a way to redefine what we view as progress. There is much to do. We addict our children to consumption and tell them you have to have the latest material things in order to be viewed as somebody. Yet we don't provide the education and training for them to get the jobs to get those things legally. We've also told rich kids that they need all those things, and they're finding that their appetites aren't really satisfied. So we have a spiritual poverty problem. [T]hat is going to have to be confronted in a culture that treats children as consumers, rather than as developing human beings in need of protection.

Race plays a big role in lots of complicated ways. It has been the tradition for powerful southerners to use race as a way of dividing the poor white and black citizens. [T]here are more poor white children and families who are struggling, more poor whites who are hungry, and more poor whites without health insurance. [However], in their own minds, they have had poverty defined as something that is about "those other people"—black people and brown people. Many powerful, wealthy interests sought to maintain control and power by keeping folks divided, and [by] making poor whites feel that somehow they were much better because of that white skin. And so there was always an economic underpinning to racism that in many ways continues, and that is very sad. The issues of children, race, and poverty are intertwined.

We have made a conscious effort over the last twenty-five years to try to redefine the face of the poor and hurting child. Black and brown children have a disproportionate chance of being poor and being at risk of all the worst things. Still, in numbers, there are more poor whites. We constantly try to say that the majority of children who are affected are white, and we always try to get white welfare recipients to testify so that the congresspeople realize this can happen to somebody they identify with. But there is such a long history of stereotyping that it is very difficult not to have people constantly put a black face on poverty.

Being black makes it much harder to beat the odds. Ninety percent of our poor, brown, black, disabled, and immigrant children are in public schools, and so many people really don't think they can learn. They think it's pouring good money into bad vessels. And there are few school systems in America where all children are expected to learn and are supported in learning. As a result, the children who need the most get the least. They get the poorest schools, the poorest teachers, the poorest labs, the poorest books, and that's racism. Although we have made great progress, it is still harder to be both poor and black. And if you look at life expectancy, or poverty, or violence, blacks are disproportionately victimized. We once did a sheet showing if you are a black male in America, you are far more likely to be killed than people in many other countries. We couldn't get it all on one page. We just folded it out to compare it with violence and death rates in other countries. So race is still a real problem.

The first time I walked into a federal court in Mississippi, there were all these white male lawyers sitting around a table, and not a single one would speak or shake hands. I knew who I was and I had a job to do, but there were times when I was absolutely terrified. I happened to have been in Mississippi the first day that police dogs were brought out against civil rights demonstrators. I was trying hard not to get arrested because I knew my ability to get into the Mississippi bar was at stake. I watched in terror and awe as [civil rights activists] Bob Moses and Jim Forman and others, including old people, were attacked and scattered by these dogs. But Bob didn't move. To watch their courage on a daily basis just gives you enough to think, "What are you complaining about?"

I am also clear that if we do not save our children, we are not going to be able to save ourselves. We often forget that it was children who [during the civil rights movement] had to go through the mobs and weather the violence in Birmingham and Selma, children who were herded into the cattle cars and jails in Jackson. Their parents were terrified, but their children were the frontline soldiers. Look at the sacrifices of those four girls blown asunder [by the Ku Klux Klan in 1963] in Birmingham. I was blessed by the opportunity that Dr. King and the [civil rights] movement provided to feel empowered as a young person, and by how absolutely ready and prepared we were to die and to do whatever was necessary.

Courage is just hanging in there when you get scared to death. One of the things that I remember about Dr. King is how as a young person he could always look scared to death. Look at his face in many of his pictures: he is depressed. He often did not know what he was going to do next. I remember him saying how terrified he was of the police dogs in the back of the car when he was being taken out to rural Georgia after being arrested. And in my little college diary, the first time I met him, I must have written down half of the speech he gave, about how you don't have to see the whole stairway to take the first step. You can be scared but shouldn't let it paralyze you. And he used to say over and over again, "If you can't run, walk; if you can't walk, crawl; if you can't crawl, just keep moving." That reflects courage. There comes a point in life when you look around and decide that this is not what life's about. And you have to change things. And if that means dying, that's fine. Many people were terrified in the civil rights days, but terror is a part of living in an unjust system. That's courage—acting despite it all.

WANGARI MAATHAI
Kenya—Women and the Environment

Wangari Maathai, Kenya's foremost environmentalist and women's rights advocate, founded the Green Belt Movement on Earth Day 1977, encouraging the farmers (70 percent of whom are women) to plant "greenbelts" to stop soil erosion, provide shade, and create a source of lumber and firewood. She distributed seedlings to rural women and set up an incentive system for each seedling that survived. To date, the movement has planted over fifteen million trees, produced income for eighty thousand people in Kenya alone, and has expanded its efforts to over thirty African countries, the United States, and Haiti. A few years later, when Maathai denounced President Daniel arap Moi's proposal to erect a sixty-two-story skyscraper in the middle of Nairobi's largest park, officials warned her to curtail her criticism. When she took her campaign public, she was visited by security forces. When she still refused to be silenced, she was subjected to a harassment campaign and threats.

Eventually Moi was forced to forego the project, in large measure because of the pressure Maathai successfully generated. Years later, when she returned to the park to lead a rally on behalf of political prisoners, Maathai was hospitalized after pro-government thugs beat her and other women protesters. Following the incident, Moi's ruling party parliamentarians threatened to mutilate her genitals in order to force Maathai to behave "like women should." But Wangari Maathai was more determined than ever, and continued her work for environmental protection, women's rights, and democratic reform. From one seedling, an organization for empowerment and political participation has grown many strong branches.

In 2005, Maathai was selected to preside over the African Union's Economic, Social and Cultural Council. Wangari Maathai died in September 2011, while undergoing cancer treatment at the age of 71.

INTERVIEW TAKEN FROM KERRY KENNEDY'S BOOK *SPEAK TRUTH TO POWER*, 2000

> "WHEN YOU START DOING THIS WORK, YOU DO IT WITH A VERY PURE HEART, OUT OF COMPASSION... THE CLARITY OF WHAT YOU OUGHT TO DO GIVES YOU COURAGE, REMOVES THE FEAR, GIVES YOU THE COURAGE TO ASK. THERE IS SO MUCH YOU DO NOT KNOW. AND YOU NEED TO KNOW." —Wangari Maathai

The Green Belt Movement in Kenya started in 1977 when women from rural areas and urban centers, reflecting on their needs at organized forums, spoke about environmental degradation. They did not have firewood. They needed fruits to cure malnutrition in their children. They needed clean drinking water, but the pesticides and herbicides used on farms to grow cash crops polluted the water.

The women talked about how, a long time ago, they did not have to spend so much time going out to collect firewood, that they lived near the forest. They spoke of how, once, they ate food that sustained their health. Now, while the food does not require much energy to grow, it does not sustain them. The women feel their families are now very weak, cannot resist diseases, and that their bodies are impoverished because of an environment that is degraded.

The National Council of Women, a non-governmental organization, responded by encouraging them to plant trees. In the beginning it was difficult because the women felt that they had neither the knowledge, the technology, nor the capital to do this. But, we quickly showed them that we did not need all of that to plant trees, which made the tree-planting process a wonderful symbol of hope. Tree-planting empowered these women because it was not a complicated thing. It was something that they could do and see the results of. They could, by their own actions, improve the quality of their lives.

When we said we wanted to plant fifteen million trees, a forester laughed and said we could have as many seedlings as we wanted because he was convinced that we could not plant that many trees. Before too long, he had to withdraw that offer because we were collecting more trees than he could give away free of charge. But we didn't have money. We decided that we could produce the seedlings ourselves. We would go and collect seeds from the trees, come back and plant them the way women did other seeds: beans, corn, and other grains. And so the women actually developed forestry management techniques, using "appropriate technology" to fit their needs. Here is the basic method: take a pot, put in the soil, and put in the seeds. Put the pot in an elevated position so that the chickens and the goats don't come and eat the seedlings.

This method worked! Some day we will record all the inventive techniques that the women developed. For example, sometimes trees produce seeds carried by the wind. These germinate in the fields with the first rain. It was very interesting to see a woman cultivating a field with a small container of water. But, she was cultivating weeds! She had learned that among these weeds were also tree seedlings, and that she could pick the seedlings and put them in a container. In the evening, she went home with several hundred seedling trees! These techniques developed by the women became extremely helpful. We planted more than twenty million trees in Kenya alone. In other African countries, we have not kept records. Trees are alive, so we react to them in very different ways. Quite often, we get attached to a tree, because it gives us food and fodder for our fires. It is such a friendly thing. When you plant a tree and you see it grow, something happens to you. You want to protect it, and you value it. I have seen people really change and look at trees very differently from the way they would in the past. The other thing is that a lot of people do not see that there are no trees until they open their eyes, and realize that the land is naked. They begin to see that while rain can be a blessing, it can also be a curse, because when it comes and you have not protected your soil, it carries the soil away with it! And this is the rich soil in which you should be growing your food. They see the immediate relationship between a person and the environment. It is wonderful to see that transformation, and that is what sustains the movement!

We have started programs in about twenty countries. The main focus is how ordinary people can be mobilized to do something for the environment. It is mainly an education program, and implicit in the action of planting trees is a civic education, a strategy to empower people and to give them a sense of taking their destiny into their own hands, removing their fear, so that they can stand up for themselves and for their environmental rights. The strategy we use is a strategy that we call the "wrong bus syndrome," a simple analogy to help people conceive what is going on. People come to see us with a lot of problems: they have no food, they are hungry, their water is dirty, their infrastructure has broken down, they do not have water for their animals, they cannot take their children to school. The highest number of problems I have recorded at a sitting of about a hundred people is one hundred and fifty. They really think we are going to solve their problems. I just write them down, but I am not going to do anything about them. I just write them down in order to give the people a feeling of relief and a forum where they can express their problems.

After we list these problems, we ask, "Where do you think these problems come from?" Some people blame the government, fingering the Governor or the President or his Ministers. Blame is placed on the side that has the power. The people do not think that they, themselves, may be contributing to the problem. So, we use the bus symbol (because it is a very common method of transportation in the country). If you go onto the wrong bus, you end up at the wrong destination. You may be very hungry because you do not have any money. You may, of course, be saved by the person you were going to visit, but you may also be arrested by the police for hanging around and looking like you are lost! You may be mugged—anything can happen to you! We ask the people, "What could possibly make you get on the wrong bus? How can you walk into a bus station and instead of taking the right bus, take the wrong one?" Now, this is a very ordinary experience. The most common reason for people to be on the wrong bus is that they do not know how to read and write. If you are afraid, you can get onto the wrong bus. If you are arrogant, if you think you know it all, you can easily make a mistake and get onto the wrong bus. If you are not mentally alert, not focused. There are many reasons.

After we go through this exercise, we ask them to look at all the problems that they have listed. Why are we hungry? Why are we harassed by the police? We cannot hold meetings without a license. When we look at all of this, we realize that we are in the wrong bus. We have been misinformed for too long. The history of Kenya in the last forty years explains why.

During the Cold War period, our government became very dictatorial. There was only one radio station that gave out controlled information and our country was misinformed. Because the government was so oppressive, fear was instilled in us, and we very easily got onto the wrong bus. We made mistakes and created all of these problems for ourselves. We did not look at the environment and decide to plant trees, so our land was washed away by the rain! The beautiful topsoil was lost. Then, we had made the mistake. Maybe we were not fully focused, suffered from alcoholism, or were not working, but our personal problems had nothing to do with government. We got on the wrong bus and a lot of bad things happened. What we needed to do was to decide to get out, only to make the best of the situation you find yourself in.

You need to take action. You have to inform yourself. And you are willing to inquire; you are willing to learn. That is why you came to the seminar. You want to plant, you want to empower yourself. You have every right to read what you want to read. You want to meet without asking permission. To get off the bus means to control the direction of your own life.

We say to go ahead and start to plant trees. Grow and produce enough food for your family. Get in the food security project, making sure that you plant a lot of indigenous food crops so that we do not lose local biodiversity. We are working in the tropics so the trees grow very fast. In five years, or less, you can have fruit trees, like banana trees. You can go and teach others what you have learned here so that you will have educational outreach in the village. We will support you, so that you can encourage others to get off the bus. You can get a small group of people to protect a park or a forest or an open space near you. Environmental protection is not just about talking. It is also about taking action.

People who live near the forest are among the first to see that the forest is being destroyed. People who live near water resources are the ones who notice that these springs are being interfered with. People who are farmers recognize that the soil is being exposed and carried away by the rains. These are the people who should be the ones to draw attention to these problems at the local and national levels.

And this is the process I have seen with the Green Belt Movement. Women who start to plant trees on their farms influence their neighbors. The neighbors eventually become involved. At the national level, we have been able to draw the attention of the Parliament, and even the President, to the need to protect the environment! And now, we see the government reacting to what the environmentalists are saying: that the remaining forest not be degraded, that open spaces not be privatized, and that the forest not be interfered with or privatized. This pressure is coming from ordinary people. We started by empowering women. Then the men joined in because they saw that the women were doing some very positive work.

A lot of men participate in the planting, though not in the nurturing of the seedlings at the nursery as the women do (and do very well). The men see trees as an economic investment. They look thirty years into the future and see that they will have huge trees to sell. Well, nevertheless, it means that the Green Belt Movement enjoys the participation of men, women, and children, which is important. You could very easily have the women planting trees and the men cutting the trees down! Everyone needs to work together and to protect the environment together.

When you start doing this work, you do it with a very pure heart, out of compassion. Listen to the statement from our pamphlet: "The main objective of this organization is to raise the consciousness of our people to the level which moves them to do the right things for the environment because their hearts have been touched and their minds convinced to do the right things, because it is the only logical thing to do."

The clarity of what you ought to do gives you courage, removes the fear, gives you the courage to ask. There is so much you do not know. And you need to know. And it helps you get your mind focused. Now, you are out of the bus and moving to the right direction. They will see you move with passion, conviction, and persistence. You are very focused. Quite often you threaten people, either people who are on the wrong bus or people who are driving others, because you know they are driving people in the wrong direction and you are asking them not to follow. And now you feel free to tell people, "Believe me, you are all moving in the wrong direction, your leader as well." Now, of course, a leader does not want to be told this. He certainly does not want to hear the people he is driving being told they need to get out of the bus. This is where the conflict comes in. The leader accuses you of misleading his people, misrepresenting his vision, misrepresenting what he's trying to do, misrepresenting him.

This is what happened between me and President Moi. In 1989, the president wanted to take over Uhuru Park, the only park left in Nairobi. He was going to build the highest building in Africa, sixty-two stories. Next to the skyscraper he was going to put a four-story statue of himself (so you could pat his head from the fourth floor). All of downtown Nairobi would have had to be restructured.

That building would have been so intimidating, that even if some land in the small park remained, no one would have dared come near it. Very intimidating. So it was completely wrong. It also would have been an economic disaster, as was borrowing money to do it, putting us in greater debt. It was truly a white elephant. But he wanted it because it was a personal aggrandizement.

And so we raised objections, and said this was the only park that we had in the city where people who have no money could come. Not even a policeman could ask you to move; it was an open space. A lot of people joined in and agreed, even those people who were going to invest, who then decided that it was probably not a very good idea.

We staged a protest in the park and were beaten by the police. We were only a small group of women, because, at that time, in 1989, there was a lot of fear. I had taken the matter to court, arguing that this park belonged to the people and that it could not be privatized. The President was only a public trustee, so for him to now go and take what had been entrusted to him, to take it, and privatize it, was criminal. We

neck." The press loved it. Parliament was just being mean, chauvinistic, and downright dirty. Fortunately, my skin is thick, like an elephant's. The more they abused and ridiculed me, the more they hardened me. I know I was right, and they were wrong.

A few years later, in 1992, with about ten women whose sons had been detained for demanding more democratic rights for the people, I went back to the same park and declared it "freedom corner." We stayed there for four days. By the fifth day the government brought in policemen; some of us were very badly beaten. But I will always remember the power of those women. After we were disrupted by the police, I ended up in the hospital, so I didn't even know what was going on. The other women were herded into cars and forced to go back to where they had come. But the following day, those women came

"WHEN YOU PLANT A TREE AND YOU SEE IT GROW, SOMETHING HAPPENS TO YOU. YOU WANT TO PROTECT IT, AND YOU VALUE IT. I HAVE SEEN PEOPLE REALLY CHANGE AND LOOK AT TREES VERY DIFFERENTLY FROM THE WAY THEY WOULD IN THE PAST." –Wangari Maathai

lost the case, which in the court meant that we had no business raising the issue and complaining about the park. But we won in the end because those who were providing the money withdrew due to the outcry from the public. And members of Parliament actually suspended business to discuss the Green Belt Movement and myself, recommending that the Green Belt Movement should be banned as a subversive organization. They did a lot of dirty campaigning to discredit us, including dismissing us as, "a bunch of divorcées and irresponsible women."

Well, I gave them a piece of my mind that people kept talking about for the rest of the time. "Whatever else you may think about the women who run the Green Belt Movement," I said, "we are dealing here with privatizing or not privatizing a public park. We are dealing with the rights of the public and the rights of the people. These are the kind of issues that require the anatomy of whatever lies above the

back to Nairobi and tried to locate the others. They knew some were in the hospital, and sent a message that they were waiting for us. They would not go home. Instead, they went to the Anglican Provost of All Saints Cathedral who told them they could go to the crypt and wait for the other women. Though the Provost thought this would be a two-night stay, it lasted for one year. They stayed in that crypt, waiting for Moi to release their sons. The authorities tried everything to get the women to leave. They tried to bribe some of them; intimidated them; even sent some of their sons to persuade their mothers to leave. Several times we were surrounded by armed policemen, who threatened to break the doors of the church and to haul us out. Fortunately they never did, because some of these soldiers were Christians, and we could hear them say they just could not break into the church.

KAILASH SATYARTHI
India—Child Labor

Kailash Satyarthi is India's lodestar for the abolition of child labor. Since 1980, he has led the rescue of more than 75,000 bonded and child slaves in India and developed a successful model for their education and rehabilitation. Satyarthi has emancipated thousands of children from bonded labor, a form of slavery in which a desperate family typically borrows needed funds from a lender (sums as little as $35) and is forced to hand over a child as surety until the funds can be repaid. But often the money can never be repaid—and the child is sold and resold to different masters. Bonded laborers work in the diamond, stonecutting, manufacturing, and other industries.

They are especially prevalent in the carpet export business, where they hand-knot rugs for the American and other markets. Satyarthi rescues children and women from enslavement in the overcrowded, filthy and isolated factories where conditions are deplorable, with inhuman hours, unsafe workplaces, rampant torture, and sexual assault. Satyarthi has faced false charges and constant death threats for his work. The death threats are taken seriously—two of Satyarthi's colleagues have been murdered. He has been recognized around the world for his work in abolishing child labor. Satyarthi organized and led two great marches across India to raise awareness about child labor. On the global stage, he has been the architect of the single largest civil society network for the most exploited children, the "Global March Against Child Labor," active in more than 140 countries.

Kailash Satyarthi received the 1995 Robert F. Kennedy Human Rights Award and the 2002 Raoul Wallenberg Human Rights Award. The U.S. State Department's 2007 Trafficking in Persons Report has named him a "Hero Acting to End Modern-Day Slavery."

In 2014, Satyarthi won the Nobel Peace Prize for his struggle against the suppression of children and young people and for the right of all children to education.

INTERVIEW TAKEN FROM KERRY KENNEDY'S BOOK *SPEAK TRUTH TO POWER*, 2000

"SMALL CHILDREN OF SIX, SEVEN YEARS AND OLDER ARE FORCED TO WORK FOURTEEN HOURS A DAY, WITHOUT BREAKS OR A DAY OF REST. IF THEY CRY FOR THEIR PARENTS, THEY ARE BEATEN SEVERELY, SOMETIMES HANGED UPSIDE DOWN FROM THE TREES AND EVEN BRANDED OR BURNED WITH CIGARETTES." —Kailash Satyarthi

Bonded labor is a form of modern-day slavery, where ordinary people lose the most basic freedom of movement, the freedom of choice. They are forced to work long hours with little rest. Over five million children are born into such slavery. Their parents or grandparents may have borrowed a petty sum from a local landlord and consequently generations and generations have to work for the same master. They are prisoners—forbidden to leave. Another five million children are sent to work when their parents receive a token advance and this small amount is used to justify unending years of hardship.

The conditions of bonded labor are completely inhuman. Small children of six or seven years and older are forced to work fourteen hours a day, without breaks or a day of rest. If they cry for their parents, they are beaten severely, sometimes hanged upside-down from the trees and even branded or burned with cigarettes. They are often kept half-fed because the employers feel that if they are fed properly, then they will be sleepy and slow in their work. In many cases they are not even permitted to talk to each other or laugh out loud because it makes the work less efficient. It is real medieval slavery.

We believe that no other form of human rights violation can be worse than this. This is the most shameful defeat of Indian law, our country's constitution and the United Nations Charter. Our most effective armor in this situation is to educate the masses and to create concern and awareness against this social evil. In addition, we attempt to identify areas where child slavery is common. We conduct secret raids to free these children and return them to their families. Follow-up on their education and rehabilitation is an equally vital step in the whole process.

We lobby different sectors of society, parliamentarians, religious groups, trade unions, and others, who we believe could influence the situation. We have about a hundred full-time and part-time associates in our group. But we have also formed a network of over 470 non-governmental organizations in India and other South Asian countries.

For us, working with enslaved children has never been an easy task. It very often involves quite traumatic situations. These children have been in bondage ever since the time they can remember. Liberty for them is an unfamiliar word. They don't know what it is like to be "free." For us, the foremost challenge is to return to them their lost childhood. It is not as simple as it might sound—we really have to work hard at it. For instance, one of the children we've freed was a fourteen-year-old boy, Nageshwar, who was found branded with red-hot iron rods. Coincidentally, at that time, an official from the RFK Center for Human Rights was in India and she came across the boy in New Delhi. The trauma Nageshwar went through had made him lose his speech. He was even unable to explain his condition. It was only later through other children that we came to know about what had happened to him. We really have to work hard to reach such children.

As you may be well aware, marches and walks have been an integral part of our Indian tradition. Mahatma Gandhi marched several times to educate the people (and also to learn something himself!). Keeping in view their strong impact, especially when it comes to mass mobilization, marches have always occupied a prominent place in our overall strategy to combat child slavery. Marching doesn't mean that we are trying to impose anything. Our demonstrations have about 200 to 250 marchers, half of whom are children—children who have been freed from bondage and slavery. They act as living examples of the dire need to educate people about both the negative impact of the bonded labor system and the positive impact of their newly gained freedom. The other marchers are representatives from human rights organizations, trade unions, and social organizations who join in solidarity. We go to different villages every day, and conduct public meetings, street theater, cultural activities, and press conferences to put across our message to the people.

Two years ago we welcomed the Prime Minister's promise to act against child labor, if not against bonded labor. We were hoping for some positive results, some impetus to reforms. But even after all this time, no action has taken place. It is very unfortunate. The pronouncement initially created some fear in the minds of employers, but now it is going to prove counterproductive to reform.

People by now realized it was nothing more than a political gimmick and that there was no real will behind it. The employees are a varied lot. When a child is bonded to a street restaurant, the employer is usually an ordinary person of some remote village or town. But when children are employed in carpet weaving, or the glass industry or the brassware industry, the employers are "big" people. They generate a lot of foreign exchange through exports and are always considered favorably by the government.

Despite this, I am not in favor of a total boycott or blanket ban on the export of Indian carpets. Instead I have suggested that consumers buy only those carpets that are guaranteed made without child labor. Consumer education is a must to generate demand for such carpets. We believe that if more and more consumers pressed this issue, more and more employers would be compelled to free child workers and replace them with adults. It is unfortunate that in the last few years in India, Pakistan, and Nepal, the numbers of children in servitude have gone up, paralleling the growth in exports. For instance, today in India we have about 300,000 children in the carpet industry alone with the export market of over U.S. $600 million a year. Ten or fifteen years ago, the number of children was somewhere between 75,000 to 100,000 and at that time the exports were not for more than U.S. $100 million. The direct relation between these two is clearly evident.

This fact compelled us to launch a consumer campaign abroad. Health and environment have been the prime concerns among the consumers in the West—in Germany, in the U.S. But the issue of children was never linked with this consumer consciousness. People thought of environment and animal rights, but they never thought about children. But in the last couple years, I am proud that the child labor issue has gained momentum and has become one of the big campaigns in the world. What began with awareness and publicity has now expanded to issues of compliance.

We have recommended the establishment of an independent and professional, internationally credible body to inspect, monitor, and finally certify carpets and other products have been made without child labor. We formed the Rugmark Foundation as an independent body with non-governmental organizations like UNICEF. They appoint field inspectors, and give all carpets a quote number that gives the details of the production history of the carpet. The labels are woven in the backside of the carpet, and nobody can remove or replace them. This is a significant step in ending this exploitation.

But even this task of educating Western consumers is not so easy. It does involve its share of risks. For example, a German TV film company, after initial research, exposed the employment of children in the carpet export industry. The story was of an importer in Germany, IKEA, who had announced that they would deal only with child-labor-free goods. So reporters started investigating. They came to my office and ashram and interviewed me. Their interview was of a very general nature but when the film was shown later it mentioned Sheena Export in detail, which resulted in the cancellation of a big order from IKEA. Sheena Export, one of the biggest players in the field, became notorious, which affected their exports to other countries, including the United States, which was worth U.S. $200 million a year. The company is politically very powerful (one of the brothers is the transport minister in the state of Haryana) and so they decided to fight back.

I know that the entire carpet industry, or the majority of it, opposes me. They believe I am their enemy; they just want to eliminate me. They wanted to take me to Haryana, the state known for the worst human rights violations, fake encounters, illegal custody, and killings of people in jail and in police stations. I was arrested on June 1. They wanted to arrest me legally, but they never informed the Delhi police, which is required under Indian law. Because the police came from another state and had no jurisdiction, they couldn't legally arrest me in my home in Delhi. But they tried. I was able to make phone calls and consult a few people on this, and finally I told them that they could not arrest me. The Haryana police did not pay any attention and threatened to break in. They took out their pistols. As you can imagine, their presence had created terror in the whole neighborhood. I was finally arrested and later released on bail. It was not the first time, though it was the first that such a big plot was cooked up against me. At times in the past I have faced such threats. Two of my colleagues have also been killed.

I think of it all as a test. This is a moral examination that one has to pass. If you decide to stand up against such social evils, you have to be fully prepared—not just physically or mentally, but also spiritually. One has to pull oneself together for the supreme sacrifice—and people have done so in the past. Robert F. Kennedy did, Mahatma Gandhi, Indira Gandhi, John Kennedy—the list can go on endlessly. Resistance—it is there always, we only have to prepare ourselves for it. We will have to face it, sooner or later. It is the history of humanity, after all.

"FOR US, WORKING WITH ENSLAVED CHILDREN HAS NEVER BEEN AN EASY TASK. IT VERY OFTEN INVOLVES QUITE TRAUMATIC SITUATIONS. THESE CHILDREN HAVE BEEN IN BONDAGE EVER SINCE THE TIME THEY CAN REMEMBER. LIBERTY FOR THEM IS AN UNFAMILIAR WORD. THEY DON'T KNOW WHAT IT IS LIKE TO BE "FREE." FOR US, THE FOREMOST CHALLENGE IS TO RETURN TO THEM THEIR LOST CHILDHOODS."—Kailash Satyarthi

ELEMENTARY

"WHAT ARE HUMAN RIGHTS?"

HUMAN RIGHTS ARE THE RIGHTS A PERSON HAS SIMPLY BECAUSE SHE OR HE IS A HUMAN BEING. Human rights are held by all persons equally, universally, and forever. Human rights are inalienable: you cannot lose these rights any more than you can cease being a human being. Human rights are indivisible: you cannot be denied a right because it is "less important" or "non-essential." Human rights are interdependent: all human rights are part of a complementary framework. For example, your ability to participate in your government is directly affected by your right to express yourself, to get an education, and even to obtain the necessities of life.

Another definition of human rights is those basic standards without which people cannot live with dignity. To violate someone's human rights is to treat that person as though she or he were not a human being. To advocate for human rights is to demand that the human dignity of all people be respected. In claiming these human rights, everyone also accepts the responsibility not to infringe on the rights of others and to support those whose rights are abused or denied.

Human rights are both inspirational and practical. Human rights principles hold up the vision of a free, just, and peaceful world, and set minimum standards for how individuals and institutions everywhere should treat people. Human rights also empower people with a framework for action when those minimum standards are not met, for people still have human rights, even if the laws or those in power do not recognize or protect them.

We experience our human rights every day when we worship according to our beliefs, or choose not to worship at all; when we debate and criticize government policies; when we join a trade union; or when we travel to other parts of the country or overseas. Although we usually take these actions for granted, people both here in America and in other countries do not enjoy all these liberties equally. Human rights violations occur when a parent abuses a child; when a family is homeless; when a school provides inadequate education; when women are paid less than men; or when one person steals from another. Human rights are an everyday issue.

ABOUT THE LESSON PLANS

THE SPEAK TRUTH TO POWER CURRICULUM INTRODUCES GENERAL HUMAN RIGHTS ISSUES THROUGH THE STORIES OF REMARKABLE PEOPLE WORKING IN THE FIELD, AND URGES STUDENTS TO BECOME PERSONALLY INVOLVED IN THE PROTECTION OF HUMAN RIGHTS.

Human rights violations are defined by international law. It is important that students have a clear idea about what is a human rights violation under the rule of law.

So what does Speak Truth To Power mean? Does it mean speaking truth to those in power or does it mean that speaking truth has power? The answer depends on how you and your students engage with this curriculum and what actions you take as a result. In reality, when truth is informed by sound learning, it has power. Likewise, those who are informed understand their obligation to speak truth to those in power.

The recognition of social justice is an important component in the emotional development of young people. The purpose of this curriculum is to support students' understanding of their global environment and the importance of standing up for your fellow citizens of the world. It is our hope that the curriculum will help students make connections between everyday activities and human rights like the right to education and fair working conditions. Through inquiry and exploration of different human rights issues, students will learn the facts around specific issues, will discover what these issues mean to them individually, how these issues affect the larger world, and what they can do to address these issues.

ADAPTING LESSONS FOR ANY GRADE LEVEL

The majority of the Speak Truth To Power lessons are written for middle and high school age learners, however, educators can use the defenders' personal narratives and adapt the lessons for learners of any age.

In all cases, first and foremost consider your students: their level of readiness and their personal experiences.

GENERAL RECOMMENDATIONS:

1. Shorten the defender stories to meet the reading level of your students.
2. Start with key vocabulary and then build into the full story.
3. Find the aspect of the story and/or the lesson that you think will most inspire your students and build from there.
4. Include a research component in order to further explore a specific human rights issue or the work of the defender.

ELEMENTARY LEVEL

For the earliest learners, we recommend:

1. Highlighting specific articles of the UDHR that are age and developmentally appropriate. Using the simplified version of the UDHR, you can discuss education, voting, work, shelter—the list is limitless.
2. Highlighting the positive behaviors and characteristics of the defenders such as taking responsibility, courage, faith, community, helping others, fairness and justice to name a few.
3. Build age and developmentally-appropriate vocabulary from the defender stories.

UNIVERSITY LEVEL

Human rights is not a subject widely taught in most schools so it is possible that students at the university level have no or limited exposure to formal human rights education. Students may have experience outside of the classroom with organizations such as Amnesty International or issue specific groups.

For university-level learners, we recommend:

1. Introducing questions and content that requires a higher level of analysis, a deeper exploration of the evolution of human rights in general and specific to the rights addressed by a defender.
2. Tease out the relationship between economic, social and cultural rights (rights that address conditions to meet the basic needs of human beings) and civil and political rights (liberty-oriented rights).
3. Examine the role of national, regional and international enforcement mechanisms and bodies.

If you have any questions or would like to brainstorm an adaptation, please feel free to contact Karen Robinson at robinson@rfkhumanrights.org.

"EACH TIME A MAN STANDS UP FOR AN IDEAL, OR ACTS TO IMPROVE THE LOT OF OTHERS, OR STRIKES OUT AGAINST INJUSTICE, HE SENDS FORTH A TINY RIPPLE OF HOPE, AND CROSSING EACH OTHER FROM A MILLION DIFFERENT CENTERS OF ENERGY AND DARING THOSE RIPPLES BUILD A CURRENT WHICH CAN SWEEP DOWN THE MIGHTIEST WALLS OF OPPRESSION AND RESISTANCE."

—Robert F. Kennedy

LOUNE VIAUD
Haiti – Needs and Wants

Loune Viaud, of Zanmi Lasante in Haiti advocates that health, access to medicine, and clean water are fundamental rights. The Haitian Constitution guarantees the right to health and education, but the government could not always deliver health or education services. Viaud's work in Haiti became even more urgent after Haiti was devastated by an earthquake. Viaud has since worked to provide health care to the most vulnerable populations and established a shelter for orphaned and abandoned children. In 2002, she won the Robert F. Kennedy Human Rights Award and in 2003 was named one of *Ms.* magazine's "Women of the Year".

> "EVERYONE, AS A PERSON ON THIS PLANET, HAS THE RIGHT TO HAVE HER AND HIS BASIC NEEDS MET, AND SHOULD HAVE WHATEVER IT TAKES TO LIVE WITH PRIDE, AND BECOME THE PERSON HE OR SHE WANTS TO BE. EVERY COUNTRY OR GROUP OF COUNTRIES SHOULD DO EVERYTHING THEY POSSIBLY CAN TO MAKE THIS HAPPEN." —Loune Viaud

There are many reasons for me to feel honored today. In the 21st century, the hard job of making sure everyone feels represented should not be taken lightly.

Who among us can say they speak for the poor or for those who have their rights abused? As honored as I am to receive this distinguished prize, I do not claim to speak for all those fighting for human rights. What I can say with confidence, however, is that I represent a group of people, many of them Haitians and many of them not, who are fighting for the rights of the poor just to survive. This is our human rights struggle, a struggle we believe to be ignored by many, even some within the human rights community.

Do the sick deserve the right to health care? Do the naked deserve the right to clothing? Do the homeless deserve the right to shelter? Do those who can't read or write deserve the right to education? The group I represent is Haitian, American, Russian, Mexican, and Peruvian. It is the family that makes up Partners In Health, the group I have served and helped to build for all of my adult life. We all believe the answer to each of these questions is a loud YES. Martin Luther King is credited with saying that "of all the forms of inequality, injustice in health is the most shocking and the most inhumane." The struggle for health and human rights is only part of our struggle, because we believe that the poor must be respected when they say, as they so often do, "we want to see health, education, and welfare (including water) as our birthrights." These basic rights must be part of being human.

As a Haitian woman who has personally seen what it means to be poor and sick, I know that we can all do better. We can move from the way things are, where the bottom billion is simply struggling not to suffer, to be as we say in Haiti, *kapab pa soufri*, to a place in which *tout moun se moun*. Everyone is a person. We are all human.

It was with great sadness that I read last week about the trouble of the over 200 Haitian refugees. Haitians who come to the United States should be treated fairly and equally. That they are singled out for such treatment is not right. Over the centuries there have been refugees from Haiti for many years, those fleeing slavery, war, dictatorships. In recent years, as Senator Kennedy noted, the U.S. administration has blocked support to my people. We need friends in this city in order to take on the root causes of much of our recent suffering. My country has the highest HIV rate in the Western Hemisphere. Not only do these restrictions deny Haitians their fundamental human right to health, but it also denies many their right to life.

Robert F. Kennedy once said: "the obligation of free men is to use their opportunities to improve the welfare of their fellow human beings." If RFK was alive, he would help the Haitian people to improve their lives.

What is a Need? What is a Want?
TOPIC: NEEDS AND WANTS

GRADE LEVEL: KINDERGARTEN

OBJECTIVE:
- To introduce the students to the concepts of need and want
- To begin to support the students' discovery of the difference between need and want

MATERIALS:
- Chart paper (divided in half length-wise) or a
- Venn Diagram structure (see below; on paper or made from string or hula hoops)

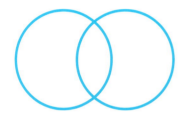

- Images of needs and wants that are similar to the images below (or photocopy the images below). You can find these in magazines or online.

DISCUSSION & ACTIVITY:
1. Ask the students to sit in a circle. Begin by asking the students what the word want means. Then ask the students what the word need means. Ask the students if they notice a difference between the two words.
2. Pass around the bag or bucket of laminated images and ask each child to choose one.
3. Go around the circle and ask each student what image they are holding. Then ask each student if the image they are holding is a need or a want.
4. Place each image on the structure under the designation each student gives.
5. Look at the chart with the students and invite their comments and observations.

CONCLUSION:
Support the students as they draw the conclusion that wants and needs are different.

LITERATURE EXTENSION:
The Universal Declaration of Human Rights: An Adaptation for Children
By Ruth Rocha and Otavio Roth
New York: United Nations Publications, 1995.

TEACHER NOTE:
Many of the cards represent things that are needs or wants depending on location.

LUCAS BENITEZ
United States – Right to Work

Lucas Benitez, of the Coalition of Immokalee Workers based in Florida, leads the fight to end exploitation on American farms. Benitez lobbies the fast food industry for a livable wage and an end to farmworker enslavement. Farming is a multi-billion-dollar industry and corporations purchase mass quantities of food for the lowest possible prices. To maintain profits, farm workers' wages have been significantly reduced and their rights are not protected. In 2003, Benitez and CIW were given the Robert F. Kennedy Human Rights Award.

> "WHAT BRINGS US TOGETHER IS A FEELING THAT WE ALL HAVE IN COMMON, SOMETHING DEEPLY ROOTED IN OUR HUMANITY—WE ARE ALL DISGUSTED BY THE FACT THAT FUNDAMENTAL HUMAN RIGHTS CONTINUE TO BE VIOLATED IN THIS DAY AND AGE IN THIS GREAT COUNTRY." –Lucas Benitez

I must tell you that today my friends and I feel a little mixed-up, as if we were lost in a sort of dream world where you can no longer know just what is real. Just two days ago, we marched into downtown Miami surrounded by nearly 3,000 police—police in riot gear, police on bicycles, police on foot, police in helicopters flying above Miami's buildings, all because we were there to call for fair trade that respects human rights, not free trade that hurts human beings. Yet today, we stand here in this historic city—in the heart of the U.S. government—receiving this incredible award for our work in defense of human rights. Truth is, my friends and I are confused. It's hard for us to understand in which of the two worlds we actually live—in the world where the voice of the poor is feared and protest in defense of human rights is considered the worst of threats to public safety?

Or in the world where the defense of human rights is celebrated and supported in the quest of a more just and fair society? While this question may well be the most difficult and important question that we must face in this new century, there is no doubt about how Robert F. Kennedy would answer were he still with us today. He—like that other great hero who was torn away from us 35 years ago, Dr. Martin Luther King—would have been there with us in the streets of Miami, probably feeling the same fear we felt facing such overwhelming force ordered against us, but continued to go forward by faith and by his powerful commitment to social justice. This award today demonstrates Robert Kennedy's vision, his belief that we as workers and poor people also are part of this democracy, that our voices must be a part of this country's great chorus and our interests taken into consideration because without justice, true peace, lasting peace, is not possible.

We are united here despite our different lives and points of view. What brings us together is a feeling that we all have in common, something deep inside of all of us—we are all disgusted by the fact that basic human rights continue to be violated in this day and age in this great country.

Behind the shiny, happy images supported by the fast-food industry with its never-ending commercials on TV, powered by over $3 billion in advertising every year, and behind the supermarket advertising that celebrates our large harvest each Thanksgiving, there is another reality. Behind those images, the reality is that there are farmworkers who give their sweat and blood so that enormous businesses can make money, all the while living in terrible conditions, with hardly any money, without the right to overtime or protection when we organize. Others are working by force, against their will, terrorized by violent employers, under the watch of armed guards, held in modern-day slavery. The right to a just wage, the right to work free of forced labor, the right to organize—three of the rights in the United Nations' Universal Declaration of Human Rights—are regularly violated when it comes to farm workers in the United States. Is this the true face of democracy in the 21st century? Is this all we can hope for our future and for our children's future? We answer from the bottom of our hearts: NO! We can—we must—hope for a better world, because a better world IS possible!

As Robert F. Kennedy said, "Some see the world as it is today and ask why. I see the world as it could be and ask, why not?" His vision of 35 years ago is not lost—we of the Coalition of Immokalee Workers are marching toward that vision today.

How are Farm Workers Paid for their Work?
TOPIC: RIGHT TO WORK

GRADE LEVEL: THIRD GRADE

OBJECTIVE:
To teach the students what the federal minimum wage is and how much it is at this time. To utilize students' math skills to figure out how much farm workers, on average, make each day.

MATERIALS:
- Paper
- Calculators, optional
- Pencils
- Activity Page "Figuring Farmworkers' Wages"
- Large Bucket (which could hold 32 pounds)
- 1 tomato

PROCEDURE:
Write $7.25 on the board. Explain to the students that this is the federal minimum wage. Further explain that even though it is a federal law not everyone makes that much. Many people make more but many more people make less than the minimum wage. Most Americans work for 8 hours a day.

DISCUSSION:
1. Hold up the tomato and the bucket. Ask the students how many tomatoes they think can fit in the bucket. Record ideas. Explain that the statistics you are going to use for the purpose of this lesson are based on average counts.
2. Explain that about 128 tomatoes can fit in the bucket. Explain to the students that they are going to figure out some math word problems using facts about farmworkers.

ACTIVITY:
Distribute the activity page to the students and review the directions. Students can work alone or in pairs to solve each problem. Remind them to show their work and be prepared to explain how they got their answers.

CONCLUSION:
Share the students' work. Ask the students what they learned about farmworkers through this activity.

Figuring Farmworkers' Wages

Use the facts listed below to help you solve the word problems.
- **AVERAGE BUCKET = 32 POUNDS**
- **4 TOMATOES = 1 POUND**
- **FARMWORKERS WORK FOR 12 HOURS A DAY**
- **$7.25 IS THE FEDERAL MINIMUM WAGE**
- **FARMWORKERS PICK ABOUT 100 TOMATOES AN HOUR**
- **FARMWORKERS ARE PAID 45 CENTS A BUCKET**

1. How much money does an average American make each day, if they receive the federal minimum wage?
2. How long does it take a farmworker to pick one bucket of tomatoes?
3. How many buckets of tomatoes can a farmworker pick in one day?
4. If a farmworker fills 10 buckets how much money would they receive?
5. If a farmworker fills 17 buckets how much money would they receive?
6. Do you think a farmworker would get paid for half a bucket?

What is a Farmworker? How do They Live?
TOPIC: RIGHT TO WORK

OBJECTIVE:
1. To help students understand the day-to-day life of a farmworker
2. To help students learn more facts about farmworkers' existence

MATERIALS:
- "Farmworker Factsheet" saf-unite.org/content/united-states-farmworker-factsheet
- Fair Food Project Videos www.youtube.com/watch?v=AIH7-O1jOx0
- Pencils
- Article 23 poster

PROCEDURE:
Distribute copies of the "Facts about Farmworkers" to the students and invite them to read silently. Encourage them to take notes or mark the page when they have a question or a comment.

DISCUSSION:
1. Ask the students what they learned about farmworkers from their reading. How does it compare to what they explored in the previous lesson?
2. Watch the Fair Food Project video. Talk about what the students observed in the video.

ACTIVITY:
Give each student a fresh piece of paper. Ask them to write, draw, diagram (their choice) the basic needs of a human being. Are farmworkers able to meet their basic needs?

CONCLUSION:
Ask the students how things should change to help support Article 23—make a list of ideas.

"YOU HAVE THE RIGHT TO WORK AND TO CHOOSE YOUR JOB, TO HAVE FAIR AND SAFE WORKING CONDITIONS, AND TO BE PROTECTED AGAINST NOT HAVING WORK. YOU HAVE THE RIGHT TO THE SAME PAY AS ANYONE ELSE WHO DOES THE SAME WORK, WITHOUT ANYONE PLAYING FAVORITES. YOU HAVE THE RIGHT TO DECENT PAY SO THAT YOU AND YOUR FAMILY CAN GET BY WITH PRIDE. THAT MEANS IF YOU DON'T GET PAID ENOUGH TO DO THAT, YOU SHOULD GET OTHER KINDS OF HELP. YOU HAVE THE RIGHT TO FORM OR TO BE PART OF A UNION THAT WILL SERVE AND PROTECT YOUR INTERESTS."—Lucas Benitez

"EACH NATION HAS DIFFERENT OBSTACLES AND DIFFERENT GOALS, SHAPED BY THE VAGARIES OF HISTORY AND OF EXPERIENCE. YET AS I TALK TO YOUNG PEOPLE AROUND THE WORLD I AM IMPRESSED NOT BY THE DIVERSITY BUT BY THE CLOSENESS OF THEIR GOALS, THEIR DESIRES AND THEIR CONCERNS AND THEIR HOPE FOR THE FUTURE."

—Robert F. Kennedy

ACTIVITIES FOR THOUGHTFUL REFLECTION

ALPHABET BOOK
Students brainstorm words or phrases about the project that begin with different letters of the alphabet. For example, with a project that develops a community garden they might think of ants (in the soil) for A, shovel for S, dig for D and then construct a book with the words in alphabetical order. The book can then be used to share the project with parents or other classes.

AWARDS
Student partners design awards for each other reflecting their work on the project. They create a certificate for their peers and share them as a whole class so each student is recognized for their contribution.

BOOKMARKS
Written or pictoral reflection is presented by each student. Students then draw or write reflections on both sides of the bookmark. Laminate the bookmark when completed.

CARTOON STRIPS
Students draw a single or multiple panel cartoon strip which explains the steps of the project they participated in and/or reflects how they feel about the steps of the project they are working on.

CLOTHESLINE
A clothesline is strung across the room. Children are given a paper t-shirt and asked to design a logo or scene that shows the student's feelings about the project. They may work either individually or as a group. The shirts are then hung on the line and shared with the class.

COLLAGE
Draw, paint, or paste together pictures or words clipped from magazines or newspapers associated with the project. Students can work independently, in pairs, or in groups.

FLAG
Children work in groups or with a partner to design their own flag that represents some part of their project. The children explain the meaning of their flag to the class.

FLOWER GARDEN
Students will be given colored paper printed with the petals of a flower, a popsicle stick, and a round cut of another color. Students will then write words or phrases on the petals, cut them out, and paste them around the round piece of paper. Popsicle sticks will be attached as stems and the flowers will be displayed in the room or on a bulletin board.

HAIKU
Poems following the 5-7-5 syllable format can be written about the project.

MOBILES OR FLIPBOOKS
This activity can be used at any point in the project. Students construct a mobile during the project depicting some aspect of the project or their feelings about it. Examples would include one at the beginning about the community the students are working with, in the middle one might show the progression of their project, and at the end there might be one that depicted an evaluation of the project's effectiveness.

NEWSPAPER OR NEWSLETTER
Students develop a newspaper or newsletter announcing the service project or interviewing students involved in the project. Topics could include feelings about impact on community and students, others' reactions, or progress reports. Newsletters could then be distributed to others, put online, and taken home to families.

OBJECT REFLECTION
The facilitator chooses various objects (rocks, paper bags, toothpicks, remote control, etc.) and places all objects on a table. Students choose an object they feel represents their projects in some way and share why they chose the object.

POETRY/SONG
Individually or as a group, students write a rap, song, or poem reflecting upon their experiences up to the point when the service project has extended. Students may perform for the rest of the class and additional verses may be added as the project progresses.

REFLECTION CENTER
A reflection center is set up in the room. Open-ended questions, and a tape recorder with a microphone, or a laptop are provided. Students can record their responses and later the class can listen to each other's reflections and discuss the results.

SIDE BY SIDE JOURNALING
During a partnership project, students from different classes or grades can journal together periodically. One student might draw while the other student writes. They then can share their thoughts with their peers in small groups.

STAND IN ANOTHER'S SHOES
Have the students choose characters or identities related their project such as an elderly person, a tree, or a bag of food. Trace two feet onto a piece of paper. Place the paper on the floor and have students step onto the feet. Students will then describe that person or object's point of view. This should be modeled for young students.

TALKING BATON
Students and teacher(s) sit in a circle. The teacher poses an open-ended question about the project to the group and hands a baton (or ball or another small object) to a student who wants to respond. The baton is then passed along until everyone has had an opportunity to share their thoughts or ideas about the question.

TIMELINE FOR CARING & SHARING
A timeline is developed by the students and displayed in the classroom. The timeline tracks the development and implementation of the project. Students' feelings and responses are then recorded at random or at selected points throughout the project.

TREE
A tree trunk is cut out of construction paper and put on a bulletin board. The project name is written on the board or on the tree trunk and students are given leaves upon which to record impressions or reflections of the project. The leaves are then attached to the tree and may be viewed by the community.

VIDEO/TAPE
The teacher or students ask each other questions about the service project and answers are recorded on video or audio tape. The tape can then be viewed by the community.

WHAT IF I WERE…
Students are provided with an experience that helps them better understand the problem they are learning about and advocating for. For example, in a project which pairs students with a nursing home, students might place cotton in their ears and listen to a tape. Discussion would then center on how it must feel to grow old and lose hearing.

WORD FEELING POEMS
Students are asked to think of one word that they think exemplifies their feelings about the service project. They then are asked to develop a poem around the word.

YARN WEB
A ball of yarn is handed to a student who shares his thoughts about the project with the rest of the group. The student holds onto the end of the yarn and tosses the rest to another student. This student then reflects on the project, takes hold of a piece of the yarn ball and tosses it to another student. The process continues until all the students have had a chance to reflect. Discuss the connection between the "web" they have created and their projects. For younger children, the ball of yarn can just be passed or rolled and the "web" could be eliminated.

UNIVERSAL DECLARATION OF HUMAN RIGHTS
SIMPLIFIED VERSION

ARTICLE 1	All human beings are born free and equal. You are worth the same, and have the same rights as anyone else. You are born with the ability to think and to know right from wrong, and should act toward others in a spirit of friendliness.
ARTICLE 2	Everyone should have all the rights and freedoms in this statement, no matter what race, sex, or color he or she may be. It shouldn't matter where you were born, what language you speak, what religion you are, what political opinions you have, or whether you're rich or poor. Everyone should have all the rights in this statement.
ARTICLE 3	Everyone has the right to live, to be free, and to feel safe.
ARTICLE 4	No one should be held in slavery for any reason. The buying and selling of human beings should be prevented at all times.
ARTICLE 5	No one shall be put through torture, or any other treatment or punishment that is cruel, or that makes him or her feel less than human.
ARTICLE 6	Everyone has the right to be accepted everywhere as a person, according to law.
ARTICLE 7	You have the right to be treated equally by the law, and to have the same protection under the law as anyone else. Everyone should be protected from being treated in ways that go against this document, and from having anyone cause others to go against the rights in this document.
ARTICLE 8	If your rights under the law are violated, you should have the right to fair and skillful judges who will see that justice is done.
ARTICLE 9	No one shall be arrested, held in jail, or thrown and kept out of her or his own country for no good reason.
ARTICLE 10	You have the same right as anyone else to a fair and public hearing by courts that will be open-minded and free to make their own decisions if you are ever accused of breaking the law, or if you have to go to court for some other reason.
ARTICLE 11	1 If you are blamed for a crime, you have the right to be thought of as innocent until you are proven guilty, according to the law, in a fair and public trial in which you have the basic things you need to defend yourself. 2 No one shall be punished for anything that was not illegal when it happened. Nor can anyone be given a greater punishment than the one that applied when the crime was committed.

| ARTICLE 12 | No one has the right to butt in to your privacy, home, or mail, or attack your honesty and self-respect for no good reason. Everyone has the right to have the law protect him or her against all such meddling or attacks. |

ARTICLE 13
1. Within any country you have the right to go and live where you want.
2. You have the right to leave any country, including your own, and return to it when you want.

ARTICLE 14
1. Everyone has the right to seek shelter from harassment in another country.
2. This right does not apply when the person has done something against the law that has nothing to do with politics, or when she or he has done something that goes against the principles of the United Nations.

ARTICLE 15
1. You have a right to a nationality.
2. No one shall be denied her or his nationality or the right to change her or his nationality.

ARTICLE 16
1. Grown men and women have the right to marry and start a family, without anyone trying to stop them or make it hard because of their race, country, or religion. Both partners have equal rights in getting married, while married, and if and when they decide to end the marriage.
2. A marriage shall take place only with the agreement of the couple.
3. The family is the basic part of society, and should be protected.

ARTICLE 17
1. Everyone has the right to have belongings that they can keep alone, or share with other people.
2. No one has the right to take your things away from you for no good reason.

ARTICLE 18
You have the right to believe the things you want to believe, to have ideas about right and wrong, and to believe in any religion you want. This includes the right to change your religion if you want, and to practice it without anybody interfering.

ARTICLE 19
You have the right to tell people how you feel about things without being told that you have to keep quiet. You have the right to read news, and watch or listen to broadcasts or listen to the radio without someone trying to stop you, no matter where you live. Finally, you have the right to print your opinions in a newspaper or magazine, and send them anywhere without anyone stopping you.

ARTICLE 20
1. You have the right to gather peacefully with people, and to be with anyone you want.
2. No one can force you to join or belong to any group.

ARTICLE 21
1. You have the right to be part of your government by being in it, or choosing the people who are in fair elections.
2. Everyone has the right to serve her or his country in some way.
3. The first job of any government is to do what its people want it to do. This means you have the right to have elections every so often, in which each person's vote counts the same, and everyone's vote is his or her own business.

ARTICLE 22 Every person on this planet has the right to have her or his basic needs met, and should have whatever it takes to live with pride, and become the person he or she wants to be. Every country or group of countries should do everything possible to make this happen.

ARTICLE 23
1 You have the right to work and to choose your job, to have fair and safe working conditions, and to be protected against not having work.
2 You have the right to the same pay as anyone else who does the same work, without anyone playing favorites.
3 You have the right to decent pay so that you and your family can get by with pride. That means that if you don't get paid enough to do that, you should get other kinds of help.
4 You have the right to form or be part of a union that will serve and protect your interests.

ARTICLE 24 Everyone has the right to rest and relaxation, which includes limiting the number of hours he or she has to work, and allowing for holidays with pay once in a while.

ARTICLE 25 You have the right to have what you need to live a decent life, including food, clothes, a home, and medical care for you and your family. You have the right to help if you're sick or unable to work, if you're older or a widow or widower, or if you're in any other kind of situation that keeps you from working through no fault of your own.

ARTICLE 26
1 Everyone has the right to an education. It should be free, and should be required for all, at least in the early years. Later education for jobs and college has to be available for anyone who wants it and is able to do it.
2 Education should help people become the best they can be. It should teach them to respect and understand each other, and to be kind to everyone, no matter who they are or where they are from. Education should help promote the activities of the United Nations in an effort to create a peaceful world.

ARTICLE 27
1 You have the right to join in and be part of the world of art, music, and books. You have the right to enjoy the arts, and to share in the advantages that come from new discoveries in the sciences.
2 You have the right to get the credit and any profit that comes from something that you have written, made, or discovered.

ARTICLE 28 All people have the right to a world in which their rights and freedoms, such as the ones in this statement, are respected and made to happen.

ARTICLE 29
1 You have a responsibility to the place you live and the people around you—we all do. Only by watching out for each other can we each become our individual best.
2 In order for all people to be free, there have to be laws and limits that respect everyone's rights, meet our sense of right and wrong, and keep the peace in a world in which everyone plays an active part.
3 Nobody should use her or his freedom to go against what the United Nations is all about.

ARTICLE 30 Nothing in this statement says anybody has the right to do anything that could weaken or take away these rights.

MALALA YOUSAFZAI
Pakistan – Right to Education

Malala Yousafzai is a student and education activist from the town of Mingora in the Swat District of Pakistan's northwestern Khyber Pakhtunkhwa province. She is known for her activism for rights to education and for women, especially in the Swat Valley, where the Taliban had at times banned girls from attending school. In early 2009, at the age of 11–12, Malala wrote a blog under a pseudonym for the British Broadcasting Company (BBC) detailing her life under Taliban rule, their attempts to take control of the valley, and her views on promoting education for girls in the Swat Valley. The following summer, a New York Times documentary was made about her life as the Pakistani military intervened in the region, culminating in the Second Battle of Swat. Malala rose in prominence, giving interviews in print and on television, and was nominated for the International Children's Peace Prize by South African activist and Speak Truth To Power human rights defender Desmond Tutu. In October of 2009, the Taliban's attempt to assassinate Malala left her in critical condition, sparking a national and international outpouring of support. The United Nations Special Envoy for Global Education, Gordon Brown, launched a petition in her name, using the slogan "I am Malala", demanding that all children worldwide be in school by the end of 2015—a petition which helped lead to the ratification of Pakistan's first Right to Education Bill. Yousafzai was the winner of Pakistan's first National Youth Peace Prize. On July 12, 2013, to celebrate her 16th birthday and Malala Day—a day declared by UN officials, Yousafzai gave her first public speech since the shooting, highlighting the necessity of universal education at the United Nations Headquarters in New York. Yousafzai was awarded the Nobel Peace Prize on December 10, 2014, for her struggle against the suppression of children and young people, and for the right of all children to education.

"SOME PEOPLE ONLY ASK OTHERS TO DO SOMETHING. I BELIEVE THAT, WHY SHOULD I WAIT FOR SOMEONE ELSE? WHY DON'T I TAKE A STEP AND MOVE FORWARD?"–Malala Yousafzai

In the name of God, The Most Beneficent, The Most Merciful. Honorable UN Secretary General Mr. Ban Ki-moon, respected President General Assembly Vuk Jeremic, Honorable UN Envoy for Global Education Mr. Gordon Brown, respected elders and my dear brothers and sisters; today it is an honor for me to be speaking again after a long time. Being here with such honorable people is a great moment in my life.

I don't know where to begin my speech. I don't know what people would be expecting me to say. But first of all, thank you to God for whom we all are equal and thank you to every person who has prayed for my fast recovery and a new life. I cannot believe how much love people have shown me. I have received thousands of good wish cards and gifts from all over the world. Thank you to all of them. Thank you to the children whose innocent words encouraged me. Thank you to my elders whose prayers strengthened me. I would like to thank my nurses, doctors and all of the staff of the hospitals in Pakistan and the UK and the UAE government who have helped me get better and recover my strength.

I fully support Mr. Ban Ki-moon, the Secretary-General in his Global Education First Initiative and the work of the UN Special Envoy, Mr. Gordon Brown. And I thank them both for the leadership they continue to give. They continue to inspire all of us to action.

Dear brothers and sisters, do remember one thing. Malala Day is not my day. Today is the day of every woman, every boy and every girl who has raised their voice for their rights. There are hundreds of human rights activists and social workers who are not only speaking for human rights, but who are struggling to achieve their goals of education, peace and equality. Thousands of people have been killed by the terrorists and millions have been injured. I am just one of them. So here I stand.... one girl among many.

I speak—not for myself, but for all girls and boys. I raise up my voice—not so that I can shout, but so that those without a voice can be heard. Those who have fought for their rights: Their right to live in peace. Their right to be treated with dignity. Their right to equality of opportunity. Their right to be educated. Dear friends, on the 9th of October 2012, the Taliban shot me on the left side of my forehead. They shot my friends too. They thought that the bullets would silence us. But they failed. And then, out of that silence came thousands of voices. The terrorists thought that they would change our aims and stop our ambitions, but nothing changed in my life except this: weakness, fear and hopelessness died. Strength, power and courage was born. I am the same Malala. My ambitions are the same. My hopes are the same. My dreams are the same.

Dear sisters and brothers, I am not against anyone. Neither am I here to speak in terms of personal revenge against the Taliban or any other terrorist group. I am here to speak up for the right of education of every child. I want education for the sons and the daughters of all the extremists, especially the Taliban.

I do not even hate the Talib who shot me. Even if there is a gun in my hand and he stands in front of me, I would not shoot him. This is the compassion that I have learnt from Muhammad—the prophet of mercy, Jesus Christ and Lord Buddha. This is the legacy of change that I have inherited from Martin Luther King, Nelson Mandela and Muhammad Ali Jinnah. This is the philosophy of non-violence that I have learnt from Gandhi Jee, Bacha Khan and Mother Teresa. And this is the forgiveness that I have learnt from my mother and father. This is what my soul is telling me, be peaceful and love everyone.

Dear sisters and brothers, we realize the importance of light when we see darkness. We realize the importance of our voice when we are silenced. In the same way, when we were in Swat, the north of Pakistan, we realized the importance of pens and books when we saw the guns. The wise saying, "The pen is mightier than sword" was true. The extremists are afraid of books and pens. The power of education frightens them. They are afraid of women. The power of the voice of women frightens them. And that is why they killed 14 innocent medical students in the recent attack in Quetta. And that is why they killed many female teachers and polio workers in Khyber Pukhtoonkhwa and FATA. That is why they are blasting schools every day. Because they were and they are afraid of change, afraid of the equality that we will bring into our society.

I remember that there was a boy in our school who was asked by a journalist, "Why are the Taliban against education?" He answered very simply. By pointing to his book he said, "A Talib doesn't know what is written inside this book." They think that God is a tiny, little conservative being who would send girls to hell just because of going to school.

The terrorists are misusing the name of Islam and Pashtun society for their own personal benefits. Pakistan is a peace-loving, democratic country. Pashtuns want education for their daughters and sons, and Islam is a religion of peace, humanity and brotherhood. Islam says that it is not only each child's right to get education, rather it is their duty and responsibility.

Honorable Secretary General, peace is necessary for education. In many parts of the world—especially Pakistan and Afghanistan, terrorism, wars and conflicts stop children to go to their schools. We are really tired of these wars. Women and children are suffering in many parts of the world in many ways. In India, innocent and poor children are victims of child labor. Many schools have been destroyed in Nigeria. People in Afghanistan have been affected by the hurdles of extremism for decades. Young girls have to do domestic child labor and are forced to get married at an early age. Poverty, ignorance, injustice, racism and the deprivation of basic rights are the main problems faced by both men and women.

Dear fellows, today I am focusing on women's rights and girls' education because they are suffering the most. There was a time when women social activists asked men to stand up for their rights. But, this time, we will do it by ourselves. I am not telling men to step away from speaking for women's rights; rather I am focusing on women to be independent to fight for themselves. Dear sisters and brothers, now it's time to speak up.

So today, we call upon the world leaders to change their strategic policies in favor of peace and prosperity. We call upon the world leaders that all the peace deals must protect women and children's rights. A deal that goes against the dignity of women and their rights is unacceptable. We call upon all governments to ensure free compulsory education for every child all over the world. We call upon all governments to fight against terrorism and violence, to protect children from brutality and harm. We call upon the developed nations to support the expansion of educational opportunities for girls in the developing world. We call upon all communities to be tolerant—to reject prejudice based on caste, creed, sect, religion, or gender, to ensure freedom and equality for women so that they can flourish. We cannot all succeed when half of us are held back. We call upon our sisters around the world to be brave—to embrace the strength within themselves and realize their full potential.

Dear brothers and sisters, we want schools and education for every child's bright future. We will continue our journey to our destination of peace and education for everyone. No one can stop us. We will speak for our rights and we will bring change through our voice. We must believe in the power and the strength of our words. Our words can change the world because we are all together, united for the cause of education. And if we want to achieve our goal, then let us empower ourselves with the weapon of knowledge and let us shield ourselves with unity and togetherness.

Dear brothers and sisters, we must not forget that millions of people are suffering from poverty, injustice and ignorance. We must not forget that millions of children are out of school. We must not forget that our sisters and brothers are waiting for a bright peaceful future. So let us wage a global struggle against illiteracy, poverty, and terrorism and let us pick up our books and pens. They are our most powerful weapons. One child, one teacher, one pen and one book can change the world. Education is the only solution. Education First.

SPEAKING UP FOR THE RIGHT TO EDUCATION – I AM MALALA
MALALA YOUSAFZAI

GRADE LEVEL: 7–12
HUMAN RIGHTS ISSUES: FREEDOM FROM PERSECUTION, EDUCATION

UNIVERSAL DECLARATION OF HUMAN RIGHTS:
Article 3: Right to Life, Liberty, and Security of Person
Article 5: Freedom from Degrading Treatment and Punishment
Article 7: Freedom from Discrimination
Article 19: Right to Freedom and Expression
Article 26: Right to Education

GUIDING QUESTIONS:
- What are the obstacles that have an impact on girls' education and the barriers that keep girls from attending school?
- What can be done to lessen these barriers?
- What is the impact of a girls' education on a family/community?
- How has Yousafzai used her voice to stand up for her rights and the rights of others?

TIME REQUIREMENT:
80–160 minutes depending on length of video shown

OBJECTIVES:
By the end of the lesson, students will be able to:
- Discuss the importance of education and the importance of equal access to education.
- Identify the reasons that girls face barriers and discrimination in educational access.
- Describe the impact of a girl's education on the global community.
- Discuss ways they can speak for others in the same way as Yousafzai.

STUDENT SKILLS:
- Collecting Data and Statistics
- Written Expression
- Using knowledge from oral, written and online resources
- Building background knowledge

CONCEPTS:
- Global Poverty
- Courage
- Right to Education
- Compassion
- Peace
- Humanity
- Brotherhood

VOCABULARY:
- Taliban
- Advocacy
- Nobel Peace Prize
- Iman
- Swat Valley
- Pakistan
- United Nations
- Bravery
- FATA
- Pashtun
- Islam

COMMON CORE STANDARDS:
- CCSS.Math.Content.HSS.IC.A.1
- CCSS.Math.Content.HSS.IC.A.2
- CCSS.Math.Content.HSS.IC.B.3
- CCSS.Math.Content.HSS.IC.B.4
- CCSS.Math.Content.HSS.IC.B.5
- CCSS.Math.Content.HSS.IC.B.6

MATERIALS:
- Diane Sawyer's full interview on ABC
- Or full CNN interview with CNN's Christiane Amanpour

- Malala's speech to the UN on her 16th birthday video: www.cnn.com/2013/07/12/world/united-nations-malala/index.html Transcript: ibnlive.in.com/news/full- text-of-malala-yousafzais- speech-at-united-nations/406812-2.html
- Statistic sheet from "Girl Rising": girlrising.pearsonfoundation.org/downloads/GR_Curriculum_Resources_STATISTICS.pdf?pdf=GR_Curriculum_Resources_STATISTICS
- World Bank statistics sheet: siteresources.worldbank.org/EXTEDSTATS/Resources/3232763-1197312825215/EdStatsNewsletter22.pdf
- The video "The Simple Case for Investing in Girls": girlsvoices.girleffect.org/why-girls/#&panel1-1

STUDENT ACTIVITIES

ANTICIPATORY SET:
- In small groups ask students to:
  - Identify future career or college interests.
  - List the education needed to achieve their future goals.
- Have students come back together as a group and ask one member from each group to list the answers. Be sure to stress that even if a student is not college-bound the necessity for a high school diploma in today's society.
- Ask students what would have happened if they were never able to attend school, if they were unable to read or write? What if they were forced to leave school after elementary school? How would their ability to achieve their goals have changed?

ACTIVITY 1:
- Introduce the statistic that there are 32 million fewer girls than boys in primary school. (Education First: An Initiative of the United Nations Secretary General, 2012.)
- Hang blank poster paper around the room. Have students walk around to brainstorm reasons for the above statistic. Bring the class back together and write down the commonalities among groups.
- Show the video from The Girl Effect – "The Simple Case for Investing in Girls" or hand out the factsheet from Girl Rising. Write down the reasons for girls' absences shown in the video girlsvoices.girleffect.org/why-girls/#&panel1-1. Have students see how many reasons that they brainstormed were in this video. Discuss what it would be like to be a girl who was one of the statistics. Remind them of their hopes and dreams.

ACTIVITY 2:
- Remind students about the previous discussion about girls' education.
- Distribute or show page 3 of the World Bank Statistics of girls out of school: siteresources.worldbank.org/EXTEDSTATS/Resources/3232763-1197312825215/EdStatsNewsletter22.pdf
- Have students locate these areas on the map.
- Tell students there is a young human rights defender who is trying to change those statistics. Show either the 20/20 interview or CNN interview with Yousafzai.
- Engage the students in a discussion with the following questions:
  - What does it mean to have courage?
  - How is Yousafzai an example of bravery and courage?

ACTIVITY 3:
- Show the video of Yousafzai's address to the United Nations or have the students read the transcript. www.cnn.com/2013/07/12/world/united-nations-malala/index.html
- Discuss their reactions to the speech:
  - Yousafzai talks about many different concepts including: compassion, brotherhood, non-violence, peace and equality.
- Ask the students to spend some time journaling about how she expresses these concepts in her speech (students may need to have the transcript next to them for this activity).
- Have students either discuss or write about how she connects her philosophy with that of great peacemakers and advocates of non-violence.

INTERNATIONAL HUMAN RIGHTS FRAMEWORK

Since the creation of the Universal Declaration of Human Rights (UDHR) by the United Nations (UN) in 1948, many other international documents have been drafted to develop these rights further. These documents include other declarations and resolutions, as well as treaties—which are also called covenants or conventions. Countries commit to protect the rights recognized in these documents. Sometimes a specific institution is created within the UN to monitor countries' compliance.

Here are examples of relevant international documents:

- The Convention on the Rights of the Child (CRC)
    - **Article 2:** Right to be free from discrimination
    - **Article 13:** Freedom of expression
    - **Article 14:** Freedom of thought, conscience, and religion
    - **Article 28:** Right to education
- International Covenant on Civil and Political Rights (ICCPR)
- International Covenant on Economic, Social and Cultural Rights (ICESCR)
- Convention on the Elimination of All Forms of Discrimination Against Women (CEDAW)

For more information, visit the Office of the High Commissioner for Human Rights' website:
www.ohchr.org

BECOME A DEFENDER

- Review what you had discussed about Yousafzai's speech.
- Write the following quote from her speech on the board:
    - "I speak- not for myself, but for all girls and boys, I raise up my voice—not so that I can shout, but so that those without a voice can be heard."
- Discuss with the students:
    - What does it mean to be an advocate or defender?
    - How does Yousafzai exemplify what it means to be a defender?
    - What does that quote mean to you?
    - How can you raise your voice for those without a voice?
    - What can you do to become a defender?
- Have the students form Action Groups of 3-5 members.
- Ask each Action Group to identify a school, community, national and international issue they feel passionate about. Have each group write their issues on flip chart paper under the different headings: School, Community, National, International.
- Have each group select one issue they will work on over the course of a specific time period leading up to a School-Wide Day of Action.
- Students should consider the following in developing their action plans:
    1. What is the end goal? Do you want to educate your community about an issue? Do you want to change a law or policy? Do you want to publically support a human rights defender like Yousafzai?
    2. Who do you need to work with or influence to help you achieve your goal? A politician, journalist, other students, community members, school administrators?
    3. How can you reach that person or those people? What is the action your group will take? (i.e. create a public service announcement, a video, write a letter to the local newspaper, organize a letter writing campaign, bring in a speaker, etc.)
    4. What materials or resources will you need to take action?
    5. Take Action!

ADDITIONAL RESOURCES

THE MALALA FUND:
www.malalafund.org
An organization dedicated to empowering girls through education.

YOUSAFZAI, MALALA AND LAMB, CHRISTIAN. I AM MALALA: THE GIRL WHO STOOD UP FOR EDUCATION AND WAS SHOT BY THE TALIBAN:
Little, Brown & Company. N.Y. 2013.
Yousafzai's autobiography.

WASHINGTON POST REVIEW:
www.washingtonpost.com/opinions/book-review-i-am-malala-by-malala-yousafzai/2013/10/11/530ba90a-329a-11e3-9c68- 1cf643210300_story.html
A review of Yousafzai's autobiography.

"MALALA INSPIRES ADVOCACY CURRICULUM AT GEORGE WASHINGTON UNIVERSITY":
www.huffingtonpost.com/2013/10/21/malala-george-washington-university_n_4135546.html
An article about GW's creation of multimedia curriculum tools to accompany Yousafzai's book.

"DIARY OF A PAKISTANI SCHOOLGIRL":
news.bbc.co.uk/2/hi/south_asia/7834402.stm
The writings that first got Yousafzai national and international attention.

"MY CONVERSATIONS WITH MALALA YOUSAFZAI":
www.csmonitor.com/World/Global-News/2012/1011/My-conversations-with-Malala-Yousafzai-the-girl-who-stood-up-to-the-Taliban-video
An account of the day of the assassination attempt.

"A HEROIC RETURN":
www.timeforkids.com/news/heroic-return/85451
An article about Yousafzai's return to school after being attacked.

SHINING HOPE FOR COMMUNITIES:
www.shofco.org
An organization transforming the face of urban poverty in Kenya through free education.

GIRL RISING:
www.girlrising.com
A movie about girls around the world fighting for the right to an education.

MIND THE GAP:
www.uis.unesco.org/Education/Pages/mind-the-gap.aspx
An online game about gender differences in education.

UN GLOBAL FIRST EDUCATION INITIATIVE:
www.globaleducationfirst.org
A five-year initiative to accelerate progress towards the Education for All goals and the education-related Millennium Development goals.

CLINTON FOUNDATION: NO CEILINGS:
www.clintonfoundation.org/our-work/no-ceilings-full-participation-project
An effort led by Hillary Clinton at the Clinton Foundation to bring together partner organizations to evaluate and share the progress women and girls have made in the 20 years since the UN Fourth World Conference on Women in Beijing.

YOUSAFZAI'S NOBEL PEACE PRICE LECTURE:
www.nobelprize.org/nobel_prizes/peace/laureates/2014/yousafzai-lecture.html
Given December 10, 2014 at the Oslo City Hall, Norway.

JAMIE NABOZNY
United States – Anti-Bullying

Jamie Nabozny grew up in Ashland, Wisconsin, a small town located on the south shore of Lake Superior. By the time Jamie was in middle school, he found himself the target of physical violence and degrading acts by classmates. When Nabozny turned to school officials for help, he was told to expect abuse for his sexuality and to stop "acting so gay."

As the attacks continued and school staff looked on with indifference, Nabozny lost hope and moved to Minneapolis. Free at last from much of the verbal and physical violence that had dominated his young life, Nabozny realized that he was not alone. Similar acts of abuse were happening to students across the country. Nabozny decided to take a stand for his rights and the rights of his fellow students. In 1995, he took legal action against his middle school, where he had been so badly beaten by his classmates that he required abdominal surgery to undo the damage.

Although his first attempt at legal action was unsuccessful, his case drew the attention of Lambda Legal, a civil-rights oriented law firm. With their help, Nabozny took his case to a federal appeals court for a second trial. His new trial issued the first judicial opinion in American history to find a public school accountable for allowing anti-gay abuse, and the school officials liable for Nabozny's injuries. This landmark decision entitled students across the United States to a safe educational experience, regardless of their sexual identity.

Today Nabozny travels the country speaking to students and teachers about the dangers of bullying and how they can stop it in their schools and communities. Nabozny's story has been turned into a short documentary, "Bullied," produced by The Southern Poverty Law Center in 2011.

EXCERPTS FROM A SPEECH GIVEN AT BRIDGEWATER STATE UNIVERSITY, APRIL 5, 2011

"AND THIS LAST FALL WAS A TURNING POINT, I DON'T THINK JUST FOR THE LGBT MOVEMENT BUT FOR THE BULLYING MOVEMENT. BECAUSE PEOPLE STARTED SAYING, 'IF KIDS ARE KILLING THEMSELVES BECAUSE OF WHAT'S HAPPENING IN SCHOOLS WE NEED TO DO SOMETHING ABOUT THAT. IF KIDS ARE KILLING THEMSELVES BECAUSE OF OUR SOCIETY'S ATTITUDES TOWARDS THEM AND WHETHER OR NOT THEY SHOULD EXIST, WE NEED TO DO SOMETHING ABOUT THAT.'"—Jamie Nabozny

I'd like to start with telling you a little bit of what happened to me when I was in school. The harassment started when I was in seventh grade, and it started with verbal harassment as it often does. Kids were calling me 'fag' and 'queer', and why they targeted me I don't know, but they did. I wasn't interested in girls, I wasn't interested in sports, and so for a variety for reasons I was singled out and targeted. I also happened to be gay, and so the harassment started. I went into the student handbook and looked up harassment and found out what steps I was supposed to take to address the harassment and that involved telling the guidance counselor who directed me to the Principal of the school. And in the very beginning the Principal said things to me like, 'I'll take care of it', 'I'll deal with it' and nothing changed, the harassment continued.

Until one day in seventh grade I was in a bathroom with my brother and some kids actually ended up pushing us into the stalls and punching us. And I thought, "Okay, now that it's turned violent the Principal has to do something." So I went into her office and told her what happened, and she said to me, "Jaime, if you're going to be so openly gay, these kinds of things are going to happen to you." And I was shocked, I left school and was suspended for leaving school without permission. I went home and told my parents and my parents demanded a meeting with these kids and their parents. There were two of the kids, one of the moms came, my mom, my dad, me, my brother and the Principal of the middle school. And at that meeting we talked about what had happened. The Principal of the middle school actually said, "Mr. and Mrs. Nabozny, boys are going to be boys, and if your son is going to be openly gay he has to expect this kind of stuff." Well as you can imagine, that sent a green light to those kids that it was okay to continue to harass me. And from that episode, the harassment continued to escalate. I attempted to kill myself, was put into an adolescent psych ward and then was returned back to the middle school in the eighth grade.

Partially through my eighth grade year I was in a science classroom, and sitting next to two of the boys who were my biggest harassers and they started groping me and grabbing me and pushed me to the ground and pretended like they were raping me in front of the entire class. The teacher was out of the classroom. I got up, my shirt was ripped, I was crying, I ran to the Principal's office, expecting, surely she's going to do something now, it's a sexual thing and I know there's a lot of rules about sexual harassment and what you're not supposed to do in school. And she just looked at me and shook her head and said, "Jaime, if you don't have an appointment than I don't have anything to say to you." I left school, and went home and I attempted to kill myself again. I then went back to Ashland and started my freshman year in high school. And my parents tried to assure me that things would be different, the kids who were harassing me were now freshman, and the older kids wouldn't know who I was. Well, in my third week of school I was pushed into a urinal and urinated on. And when I went to tell them at the office I actually didn't even get to see the Principal. The secretary called the Principal and I was told to go home and change my clothes, and nothing was done about what happened to me. I quickly realized that I needed to figure out some survival mechanisms to get me through school.

And basically a lot of times I thought I had went

numb between my ninth grade year and the last incident that happened to me, because I really didn't show my emotions at school. I'll tell you I showed them at home, I would go home and lock myself in my room and cry, and my parents were at the end of their ropes, trying to figure out what to do and trying to help me.

So in my eleventh grade year, I had found a place to hide in the morning before school started, and that particular day I didn't hide well enough. Some kids found me, and I was sitting cross-legged on the floor and one of them kicked the books out of my hands, and said, "Get up and fight, faggot." And when I went to pick the books up, he started to kick me, and he continued to kick me and kick me until the lights in the library went on which meant that the librarian was there and at that point they took off. I had to be taken to the hospital; I had to have emergency abdominal surgery for internal bruising and bleeding. My spleen had ruptured and I had a tear in my stomach. And I knew I wasn't ever going to be safe at school and I knew I had to leave Ashland. I ended up running away to Minneapolis-St. Paul which was the only place I knew gay people existed, and figured I would be safe there. I got down there and quickly realized that there's not a lot that I could do when you're seventeen to survive on the streets, or at least not things that I was willing to do and so I called home and told my parents, "you know how bad it is for me at school, just let me live here and go back to school and be safe." And my mom said it was the hardest thing that she ever had to do, was to let me go. I was only seventeen and I had just turned seventeen at that point.

And so while I was in Minneapolis I ended up going to what was, at the time, the Gay and Lesbian Community Action Council, and I ended up meeting with their Crime Victims Advocate who happened to be a lawyer and she told me that what happened to me was wrong and it was illegal and I needed to sue my school. And I went home and I called my parents and I told them about this crazy lesbian lawyer at the Community Action Council, and her crazy ideas about suing the school. And my mom was silent for a second and I could tell she had tears in her eyes, and she said, "Jaime, you need to do this, too many kids are suffering out there. And you have the ability to stand up and fight back." And she said, "Somebody needs to say this is wrong."

And so I went back to the crazy lesbian lawyer and I said, alright, I'll do it. We ended up finding a lawyer locally; the case was initially thrown out by a federal judge and at that point Lambda Legal stepped in and took over the case and joined up with Skadden Arps, which for any of you who know, it's one of the largest law firms in the world, and it was one of their partners in the Chicago firm who was my lead attorney. And not only did he take my case, but he came out as a gay, HIV positive man to his entire firm. And he said this is the case that he wanted to be remembered for, not all of the other cases that he had done. And so, just amazing people that were working on my team.

So we won a verdict against the three Principals, and not the school district and a lot of people wanted to know, why didn't they find the school district guilty? Well Wisconsin has had a law on the books since the early 1980's that said discrimination against students based on their sexual orientation was wrong. The school had a policy, and as a district, the building and the laws were there to protect me, but the people who were in charge of making sure those laws and policies were followed through on didn't do their jobs. And ultimately I think it was the best possible outcome for the case because what this holds is that school administrators now have a personal responsibility to protect students from harassment and if they do not they can be individually be sued, much like a doctor for malpractice. I've always said I don't care why people do the right thing; they just need to do the right thing. And if it means they're afraid of losing their house or their life savings, then hey, they'll protect kids and that's what needs to happen.

The case sent a message across the country that it was not okay to allow LGBT kids to be harassed and bullied in schools. And one of the things that I think sent that message loud and clear was that there was a settlement reached for $900,000. I think the message was loud and clear that if you're going to discriminate against LGBT kids then you're going to pay the price. And I naively believed that things would change overnight. And fast-forward fifteen years. This last fall, as you saw on the news there were a lot of suicides and specifically gay suicides because of anti-gay bullying and abuse that kids were suffering. And one of the things that I think is important to realize isn't that suicides and anti-gay bullying isn't on the rise, it's just that someone started paying attention last fall. And I think it's a really important clarification to make. This has been happening for a very long time. And so I started thinking about the fact that I wanted to go back out and talk about this issue, I wanted to tell my story, I wanted to talk about bullying again.

I think there are three main things that need to happen. The first thing is prevention. If you prevent something in the first place, then you don't have to deal with it. It's a pretty simple concept that seems to be forgotten over and over in this country, however, it's going to be something that we are going to have to look at and look at seriously. And some things that I think need to happen in prevention: it needs to start early. It needs to start in grade school and earlier. We need to teach children the skill of empathy; our culture doesn't do a good job of teaching the skill, and unfortunately parents don't seem to be doing a good job of teaching the skill and the reality is that there have been studies done that say you can teach empathy.

We need a comprehensive approach to bullying. What I mean by that is we need to address all the people involved in bullying, we need to train staff, we need to get the victims help so they don't internalize the messages that they hear, we need to help the bullies to understand why they're bullying and make sure that they don't end up living a life of crime, of domestic abuse, all the things that end up happening when we don't address the issue of bullying.

I realize that there's a lot of work to be done, but I'll tell you what I'm hopeful about. We are at a turning point, and this last fall with all the media coverage that was happening, I compare that to, in a lot of ways, what happened at the turn of the Civil Rights Movement when people started getting involved and caring. And what was it? It was media coverage, for the first time they were putting on the TV's pictures of people being hosed down in the streets, beaten in the streets, and America started to care, because I believe America does have a big heart, they just need to see something to get involved. And this last fall was a turning point, I don't think just for the LGBT movement but for the bullying movement. Because people started saying, "If kids are killing themselves because of what's happening in schools we need to do something about that. If kids are killing themselves because of our society's attitudes towards them and whether or not they should exist, we need to do something about that." And so, as much as I'm here to tell you there's a huge problem in this country, I'm also here to tell you that there is hope, and I know that things are changing, and things will continue to change, but it's going to take work and it's going to take all of us.

BULLYING: LANGUAGE, LITERATURE, AND LIFE
JAMIE NABOZNY

LESSON GRADE LEVEL: 7–12
HUMAN RIGHTS ISSUE: STANDARD OF LIVING, EDUCATION, FREEDOM FROM PERSECUTION, FREEDOM FROM DISCRIMINATION

UNIVERSAL DECLARATION OF HUMAN RIGHTS:
Article 2: Freedom from Discrimination
Article 3: Right to Life, Liberty, Personal Freedom
Article 5: Freedom from Torture and Degrading Treatment
Article 25: Right to an Adequate Standard of Living
Article 26: Right to an Education

GUIDING QUESTIONS:
- What does it mean to be a bully, victim, bystander and defender?
- How does language usage contribute to our understanding of bullying, our tolerance of bullying, our comfort at stepping in to stop bullying or being a by-stander?
- How has the depiction of bullying changed throughout the years?
- What can we learn from historical portrayals of bullying?

TIME REQUIREMENT:
210 Minutes

OBJECTIVES:
After this lesson, students will be able to:
- Interpret language as a factor in perpetuating or preventing bullying.
- Identify attitudes and behaviors that are consistent with bullies, victims, by-standers, and defenders.
- Understand the impact of one person standing up to and speaking out against bullying.
- Examine, through a literary lens, factors that contribute to bullying behavior.
- Develop an understanding of personal language use as a tool to stand up to bullying.

COMMON CORE LEARNING STANDARDS:
- CCSS.ELA-LITERACY.RH.6-8.1
- CCSS.ELA-LITERACY.RH.9-10.1
- CCSS.ELA-LITERACY.RH.11-12.1
- CCSS.ELA-LITERACY.RH.6-8.4
- CCSS.ELA-LITERACY.RH.9-10.4
- CCSS.ELA-LITERACY.RH.6-8.6
- CCSS.ELA-LITERACY.RH.9-10.6
- CCSS.ELA-LITERACY.RH.11-12.6
- CCSS.ELA-LITERACY.RH.6-8.8
- CCSS.ELA-LITERACY.RH.9-10.8
- CCSS.ELA-LITERACY.WHST.11-12.8

MATERIALS:
- Text pulled from required reading list
- Student handouts: www.rfkhumanrights.org / click on Speak Truth To Power / click on "Curricula" link

VOCABULARY:
- Passive
- By-stander
- Harass
- Insecurity
- Panic
- Scared
- Rumors
- Tease
- Victim
- Intimidate
- Aggression
- Brave
- Harassment
- Coward
- Respect
- Shun
- Target
- Trust
- Wronged

CONCEPTS:
- Empathy
- Fairness
- Justice
- Values
- Cultural Norms
- Systemic Change

TECHNOLOGY REQUIRED:
Internet

STUDENT ACTIVITIES

ANTICIPATORY SET:
- Write the word Bullying on the board. Ask the students to come up and write the first thing that comes to their minds when they read that term.
- After the board is filled with the students' responses, ask the students to explain their responses.
- Ask the students the following questions:
  - What is bullying?
  - Who does bullying impact?
  - What does bullying look like?
  - What roles play out in a bullying situation?
- Identify commonalities and differences among the responses and group emerging themes.
- Present to the students the vocabulary associated with bullying and handout #1.
- Ask the students to identify commonalities and differences among the vocabulary and issues raised in the handout and the class discussion on bullying.
- Based on both discussions, have the class formulate a definition of bullying. Keep this definition posted in the classroom.
- Present the students with handout #2.
- Ask the students to write one thought about the statistics. Share with class and save for use during the culminating activity.

ACTIVITY 1:
- Provide the students with a selection of readings from course-required textbooks. Choose from books that represent a range of genres and from books that were written in an earlier time period, the classics.
- Have the students select 4 to 5 readings from the list provided.
- Individually, have students explain how the text portrays bullying. This can be from the perspective of the bully, the victim, the by-stander and the defender. Ask the students to capture attitudes, behaviors, language use, means of communicating, and actions.
- In small groups, have the students share their interpretations of the texts. Ask the students to look for similarities and differences in their reading and interpretations, ask the students to share the comparisons.

ACTIVITY 2:
Follow the same steps as Activity 1, however this time, select readings from contemporary books.

ACTIVITY 3:
- In small groups, have the students select one scene that depicts bullying from the text they have studied and reviewed.
- Ask the students to share how they would change the scene to an anti-bullying scene. Students can act out the scene, they can use spoken word, or any means they feel will best allow them to demonstrate how they would change the scene.

CUMULATIVE ACTIVITY:
- Compare responses to bullying as portrayed in the selected readings from both the earlier and more contemporary texts. Highlight the commonalities and differences.
- Reflect back on the definition of bullying from the anticipatory set. Drawing on what the students have learned about language use, words and bullying from a literary perspective, and using the class definition of bullying, have the students create "the next chapter" on bullying: How would they like to see bullying change, how would they portray bullying in their own language, in their school, through their own means of communication—art, poetry, drama, spoken word, blog.
- Present the final pieces as part of an anti-bullying program or day at the school.

EXTENSION ACTIVITY:
Have the students compare language use that portrays an aspect of bullying in novels with language used with cyberbullying.

INTERNATIONAL HUMAN RIGHTS FRAMEWORK

Since the creation of the Universal Declaration of Human Rights (UDHR) by the United Nations (UN) in 1948, many other international documents have been drafted to develop these rights further. These documents include other declarations and resolutions, as well as treaties—which are also called covenants or conventions. Countries commit to protect the rights recognized in these documents. Sometimes a specific institution is created within the UN to monitor countries' compliance.

Here are examples of relevant international documents:

- The Convention on the Rights of the Child (CRC):
    - **Article 2:** Freedom from Discrimination
    - **Article 6:** Right to Life
    - **Article 7:** Freedom from Torture, Cruel, Inhuman and Degrading Treatment
    - **Article 26:** Equal Protection of the Laws
- International Covenant on Economic, Social and Cultural Rights (ICESCR)
- Convention Against Torture and Other Cruel, Inhuman or Degrading Treatment or Punishment (CAT)

For more information, visit the Office of the High Commissioner for Human Rights' website:
www.ohchr.org

BECOME A DEFENDER

- Map your school's efforts to stop bullying through the following efforts: programs, safe spaces, reporting and support. Include both school-based and cyberbullying in your mapping exercise.
- Create a map that shows the impact of the anti-bullying programs, that highlights safe spaces for students, that provides an overview of how a student reports cases of bullying, and support systems for both the bully and the bullied.
- From what is learned from the mapping exercise, work with teachers, staff, and parents to further the efforts to stop bullying in your school. Examples of what you can do include:
    1. Have each student write and sign an anti-bullying pledge (include school-based and cyberbullying). The pledges can be displayed at varying places around the schools as a reminder of the community's commitment to a bully-free school.
    2. Create a handout to include whom you should go to and whom you should contact if you are bullied or see a bullying incident. This should include teachers, administrators, 911, the state Department of Education; if the bullying is based on race, call the U.S. Department of Education Office of Civil Rights. Include this information in the student handbook and make it visible around the school.
    3. Make sure hotlines and other safety network numbers are visible and available to all students.
    4. Share your work with the wider community. In particular, consider hosting a family and/or a community anti-bullying night. Highlight the role that parents, other family members and community members can play in creating a safer place for all children. Have all participants write and sign an anti-bullying pledge.
- Write "the next chapter" on bullying for your social media sites and to share with the *Speak Truth To Power* program. The "next chapter" can include anti-bullying posts on your social media sites, taking an active role in stopping bullying in your school, and sharing your work with the wider community.
- In writing "the next chapter" advance inclusive and community-enhancing language.

ADDITIONAL RESOURCES

JAMIE NABOZNY:
www.jamienabozny.com/Home_Page.html
This website serves as the center for Nabozny's work against bullying. Through this site, you can read testimonials, find out more about his current activities and even contact him for a possible visit to your school or town.

RFK BULLYING PREVENTION:
bullying.rfkcenter.org
A project of *Speak Truth To Power*, RFK Bullying Prevention aims to provide research-based information and resources to create safe environments that prevent bullying and other negative behaviors.

ANTI-BULLYING ACTIVIST ENCOURAGES STUDENTS TO TAKE A STAND:
www.cantonrep.com/news/x789275026/Anti-bullying-activist-encourages-student-to-take-a-stand
An article recounting Jamie Nabozny's visit with the students of McKinley High School with great student reactions to his presentation.

NOT IN OUR TOWN: LIGHT IN THE DARKNESS:
www.pbs.org/show/not-our-town-light-darkness
Not In Our Town: Light in the Darkness is a one-hour documentary about a town coming together to take action after anti-immigrant violence devastates the community. In 2008, a series of attacks against Latino residents of Patchogue, New York culminate with the murder of Marcelo Lucero, an Ecuadorian immigrant who had lived in the Long Island village for 13 years.

PATCHOGUE PLUS THREE: A LOOK BACK AT A FATAL HATE CRIME:
www.thirteen.org/metrofocus/2011/09/patchogue-plus-three-a-look-back-at-a-fatal-hate-crime/
This article from Metro Focus examines the case of Marcelo Lucero, who was killed in 2008 after being attacked by a group of teens that made a game out of attacking Latinos in their neighborhood. After this brutal attack, Marcelo's younger brother Joselo has dedicated his life to criticize the anti-immigrant violence in his hometown of Suffolk County.

IT GETS BETTER PROJECT:
www.itgetsbetter.org
The It Gets Better Project was created to show young LGBT people the levels of happiness, potential, and positivity their lives will reach—if they can just get through their teen years. The It Gets Better Project wants to remind teenagers in the LGBT community that they are not alone—and it WILL get better.

THE MEGAN MEIER FOUNDATION:
www.meganmeierfoundation.org
The mission of the Megan Meier Foundation is to bring awareness, education and promote positive change to children, parents, and educators in response to the ongoing bullying and cyberbullying in our children's daily environment.

THE GAY, LESBIAN & STRAIGHT EDUCATION NETWORK:
www.glsen.org
The Gay, Lesbian & Straight Education Network strives to assure that each member of every school community is valued and respected regardless of sexual orientation or gender identity/expression.

ADDITIONAL RESOURCES

ALEX HOLMES—TAKING A STAND: FROM BULLIED TO ANTI-BULLYING LEADER:
inspiremykids.com/2010/alex-holmes-making-a-stand-from-bullied-to-anti-bullying-leader

Alex Holmes, a teenager in England who got bullied himself, decided to take a stand. He invented a role at his school called a "Student Anti-Bullying Coordinator." Then he started organizing events, creating videos, running campaigns and getting other students involved as ambassadors, event leaders and bully "patrollers." This site features a video that tells Holmes' story as well as some ways to bring this message to a classroom or school.

GUIDELINES AND RESOURCES FOR SOCIAL AND EMOTIONAL DEVELOPMENT AND LEARNING IN NEW YORK STATE:
www.p12.nysed.gov/sss/sedl/SEDLguidelines.pdf

This guidance document aims to give New York State school communities a rationale and the confidence to address child and adolescent affective development as well as cognitive development. By attending to the students' social-emotional brain development and creating conditions where school environments are calmer and safer, teachers can teach more effectively, students learn better, and parents and community can feel pride in a shared enterprise.

NEA'S BULLY FREE: IT STARTS WITH ME:
www.nea.org/home/neabullyfree.html

The NEA's Bully Free program is a part of the NEA's Issues and Actions program that is designed to help students and teachers to prevent and deal with bullying across the U.S.

BORN THIS WAY FOUNDATION:
bornthiswayfoundation.org

Led by Lady Gaga and her mother Cynthia Germanotta, the Born This Way Foundation was founded in 2011 to foster a more accepting society, where differences are embraced and individuality is celebrated. The Foundation is dedicated to creating a safe community that helps connect young people with the skills and opportunities they need to build a braver, kinder world.

THE BULLY PROJECT:
thebullyproject.com

The Bully Project highlights solutions that both address immediate needs and lead to systemic change. Starting with the film's STOP BULLYING. SPEAK UP! call to action, The Bully Project will catalyze audience awareness to action with a series of tools and programs supported by regional and national partners.

DESMOND TUTU
South Africa – Reconciliation

Archbishop Desmond Tutu's work confronting the bigotry and violence of South Africa's apartheid system won him the Nobel Peace Prize in 1984. Born in 1931 in Klerksdorf, he graduated from the University of South Africa in 1954 and was ordained as a priest in 1960. He studied and taught in England and South Africa, and in 1975 he was appointed Dean of St. Mary's Cathedral in Johannesburg, the first black South African to hold that position. In 1978 he became the first black General Secretary of the South African Council of Churches. Outspoken against the evils of apartheid, he was vilified by friend and foe, press and politicians, yet through his extraordinary patriotism and commitment to humanity, his vision, and ultimately, his faith, he persevered. After South Africa's first democratic, non-racial elections in 1994, effectively ending eighty years of white minority rule, the new Parliament created the Truth and Reconciliation Commission, appointing Tutu as its head to lead his country in an agonizing and unwavering confrontation of the brutality of the past. His faith in the Almighty is exemplified by his belief in the Word made flesh; that the battle for the triumph of good will be won or lost, not by prayers alone, but by actions taken to confront evil here on earth.

From 2007-2013, Archbishop Tutu was the Chair of the Elders, a group of prominent world leaders who contribute their integrity and moral stature to deal with some of the world's most pressing issues. Other members include Kofi Annan, Mary Robinson, Aung San Suu Kyi, and fellow Speak Truth To Power defender Muhammad Yunus.

INTERVIEW TAKEN FROM KERRY KENNEDY'S BOOK *SPEAK TRUTH TO POWER*, 2000

"WE HAVE A GOD WHO DOESN'T SAY, 'AH . . . GOT YOU!' NO. GOD SAYS, 'GET UP.' AND GOD DUSTS US OFF AND GOD SAYS, 'TRY AGAIN.'" –Archbishop Desmond Tutu

There's a high level of unemployment in South Africa that helps fuel a serious level of crime. These things feed off one another because the crime then tends to make foreign investors nervous. And there aren't enough investors to make a significant impact on the economy so the ghastly legacies of apartheid—deficits in housing, in education, and health—can be truly addressed.

If you were to put it picturesquely, you would say this man and this woman lived in a shack before April 1994. And now, four years down the line, the same man and woman still live in a shack. One could say that democracy has not made a difference in material existence, but that's being superficial.

There are changes of many kinds. Things have changed significantly for the government, despite the restrictions on resources. The miracle of 1994 still exists and continues despite all of these limiting factors that contribute to instability. They are providing free health care for children up to the age of six and for expectant mothers. They are providing free school meals and education through elementary school. But the most important change is something that people who have never lived under repression can never quite understand—what it means to be free. I am free.

How do I describe that to you who have always been free? I can now walk tall with straight shoulders, and have this sense of pride because my dignity, which had been trodden underfoot for so long, has been restored. I have a president I love—who is admired by the whole world. I now live in a country whose representatives do not have to skulk around the international community. We are accepted internationally, in sports, etc. So some things have changed very dramatically, and other things have not changed.

When I became Archbishop in 1986, it was an offense for me to go and live in Bishopscourt, the official residence of the Anglican archbishop of Cape Town. Now we live in a village that used to be white, and nobody turns a head. It's as if this is something we have done all our lives. Schools used to be segregated rigidly, according to race. Now the schools are mixed. Yes, whites tend to be able to afford private schools. But government schools, which in the past were segregated, have been desegregated. Now you see a school population reflecting the demography of our country.

I was an advocate for sanctions and as a result, most of the white community regarded me as the man they most loved to hate. They would say, "Sanctions are going to hurt blacks." Yet South Africa was prosperous largely on the basis of cheap labor, using the iniquitous migratory labor system, where black men lived in single-sex hostels for eleven months of the year. Even my constituents were ambivalent about me. And so you had graffiti like: "I was an Anglican until I put Tu and Tu together." Some were really quite funny, like "God loves Tutu" adding, "The gods must be crazy." If looks could kill, they murdered me many times over. When I got on a plane in Johannesburg, or a train in Cape Town, the looks that I got were enough to curdle milk.

I received death threats, but that was not unexpected. If you choose to be in the struggle, you are likely to be a target. There are casualties in a struggle. Of course, it isn't nice to have threats and things of that sort. But it is par for the course.

When they threatened my children, that really upset me, that really got my goat. If somebody is intent on threatening me, that's okay. But they didn't have a modicum of decency. They could hear it wasn't me, it wasn't my wife, it was only a child on the telephone. They could have either dropped the telephone, or said, "Can you call your father, or call your mother?" But they didn't.

One threat came from a group called the "White Commando." They said that either I left the country by a certain date, or they were going to dispense with me. We told the police, who showed a sense of humor. One said, "Archbishop, why don't you do us a favor and stay in bed that day?"

I think my family would have felt that they were disloyal if they pressured me to change. I asked Leah, my wife, once, "Would you like me to keep quiet?" I have never been more wonderfully affirmed than when she said, "We would much rather be unhappy with you on Robben Island (the South African island prison where black political prisoners were jailed), than have you unhappy thinking you were free (in the sense that I had been disloyal to what I believed was God's calling to me)." Anything else would have tasted like ashes. It would have been living a lie. There is no reason to live like that. I suppose I could have been maybe part of a struggle in a less prominent position. But God took me, as they say, "by the scruff of the neck," like Jeremiah, who for me is a very attractive character because he complained: "God, you cheated me. You said I was going to be a prophet. And all you made me do is speak words of doom and judgment and criticism against the people I love very much. And yet if I try not to speak the words that you want me to speak, they are like a fire in my breast, and I can't hold them in."

Now you can't believe it's the same country. The pleasures of conforming are very, very great. Now it's almost the opposite. I mean on the street, they stop to shake hands and talk. When we found out that I had cancer, I was getting cards from the most unlikely quarters. At least on one occasion a white woman wanted to carry my bags and her family gave up their seats for me. It's a change, yes, it's almost like we are in a different country.

Our country knew that it had very limited options. We could not have gone the way of the Nuremberg trial option because we didn't have clear winners and losers. We could have gone the route of the blanket amnesty and said wipe the slate clean. We didn't go either way. We didn't go the way of revenge, but we went the way of individual amnesty, giving freedom for truth, with people applying for forgiveness in an open session, so that the world and those most closely involved would know what had happened.

We were looking particularly to the fact that the process of transition is a very fragile, brittle one. We were saying we want stability, but it must be based on truth, to bring about closure as quickly as possible.

We should not be scared with being confrontational, of facing people with the wrong that they have done. Forgiving doesn't mean turning yourself into a doormat for people to wipe their boots on. Our Lord was very forgiving. But he faced up to those he thought were self-righteous, who were behaving in a ghastly fashion, and called them "a generation of vipers."

Forgiveness doesn't mean pretending things aren't as they really are. Forgiveness is the recognition that a ghastliness has happened. And forgiveness doesn't mean trying to paper over the cracks, which is what people do when they say, "Let bygones be bygones." Because they will not. They have an incredible capacity for always returning to haunt you. Forgiveness means that the wronged and the culprits of those wrongs acknowledge that something happened. And there is necessarily a measure of confrontation. People sometimes think that you shouldn't be abrasive. But sometimes you have to be to make someone acknowledge that they have done something wrong. Then once the culprit says, "I am sorry," the wronged person is under obligation, certainly if he or she is a Christian, to forgive. And forgiving means actually giving the opportunity of a new beginning.

It's like someone sitting in a dank room. It's musty. The windows are closed. The curtains are drawn. But outside the sun is shining. There is fresh air. Forgiveness is like opening the curtains, opening the window, letting the light and the air into the person's life that was like that dank room, and giving them the chance to make this new beginning. You and I as Christians have such a wonderful faith, because it is a faith of ever-new beginnings. We have a God who doesn't say, "Ah...Got you!" No, God says, "Get up." And God dusts us off and God says, "Try again."

In one instance, I was preaching in a posh church of some of the elite in the white Afrikaner community, a Dutch Reformed church, and I was probably the first black person to have done so.

I spoke about some of the things we had uncovered in the Truth and Reconciliation Commission. For instance, the previous government had had a chemical and a biological warfare program which was not just defensive, and had been looking for germs that would target only black people. They wanted to poison Nelson Mandela so that he didn't survive too long after he was released from prison. One of the ministers in the church came and joined me in the pulpit, and broke down, saying he had been a military chaplain for thirty years and didn't know these things. He hoped he'd be forgiven and I embraced him. There are others who have been less than forthright, but generally you have had people say, "We are sorry." Most of our people are ready to forgive.

There are those who are not ready to forgive, like the family of Steve Biko. That demonstrates that we are dealing with something that is not facile. It is not cheap. It is not easy. To be reconciled is not easy. And they make us so very aware of that.

One of the extraordinary things is how many of those who have suffered most grievously have been ready to forgive—people who you thought might be consumed by bitterness, by a lust for revenge. A massacre occurred in which soldiers had opened fire on a demonstration by the ANC (African National Congress), and about twenty people were killed and many wounded. We had a hearing chock-a-block full with people who had lost loved ones, or been injured. Four officers came up, one white and three black. The white said: "We gave the orders for the soldiers to open fire"—in this room, where the tension could be cut with a knife, it was so palpable. Then he turned to the audience and said, "Please, forgive us. And please receive these, my colleagues, back into the community." And that very angry audience broke out into quite deafening applause. It was an incredible moment. I said, "Let's keep quiet, because we are in the presence of something holy."

RECONCILIATION
ARCHBISHOP DESMOND TUTU

LESSON GRADE 9-12
HUMAN RIGHTS ISSUE: JUSTICE

UNIVERSAL DECLARATION OF HUMAN RIGHTS:
Article 6: Right to Recognition as a Person before the Law
Article 7: Right to Equality before the Law
Article 8: Right to Remedy by a Competent Tribunal

GUIDING QUESTIONS:
- What approaches are used to resolve conflict?
- What needs to be in place for reconciliation to be successful?

TIME REQUIREMENT:
80 minutes

OBJECTIVES:
After this lesson, students will be able to:
- Know who Archbishop Desmond Tutu is and why he is a Nobel Prize recipient and human rights defender.
- Distinguish between different approaches to achieving justice and resolving conflict.
- Advance peaceful means to conflict resolution.

COMMON CORE LEARNING STANDARDS:
- CCSS.ELA-LITERACY.RH.6-8.2
- CCSS.ELA-LITERACY.RH.6-8.4
- CCSS.ELA-LITERACY.WHST.6-8.7
- CCSS.ELA-LITERACY.WHST.6-8.9

VOCABULARY:
- Reconciliation
- Apartheid
- Afrikaner
- Patriotism
- Restorative justice
- Repression
- Post-conflict
- Revenge
- Genocide
- Amnesty
- African National Congress

CONCEPTS:
- Justice
- Human rights
- Individual Responsibility

TECHNOLOGY REQUIRED:
Internet Access

TEACHER TIP:
- Students should have an introduction to at least one case of internal conflict, political or ethnic.
- This lesson should be taught after students have studied the post-World War II and global issues.

MATERIALS:
- Interview with Desmond Tutu from *Speak Truth To Power* www.rfkhumanrights.org / click on Speak Truth To Power / click on "Curricula" link
- Desmond Tutu: Hope in Troubled Times
  www.YouTube.com/watch?v=ILCdwJj37iw
- Desmond Tutu: Truth and Reconciliation:
  www.youtube.com/watch?v=g6tJQRxxGTM

STUDENT ACTIVITIES

ANTICIPATORY SET:
- Ask students to read the interview with Archbishop Tutu and view "Desmond Tutu: Truth and Reconciliation": www.rfkhumanrights.org / click on Speak Truth to Power / click on "Curricula" link and www.youtube.com/watch?v=g6tJQRxxGTM. In this lesson, students will gain a greater understanding of ways to resolve conflict.
- After reading the interview and viewing the video, conduct a class discussion based on these questions:
    Interview:
    - How does Archbishop Desmond Tutu define forgiveness?
    - What examples of forgiveness does he write about?

    Video:
    - What are the three ways the Archbishop gives as examples on how to deal with post-conflict reconciliation? Give your interpretation of each example.
    - What did Archbishop Tutu mean when he said, "The past refuses to lie down quietly," with regard to reconciliation after apartheid was outlawed?

ACTIVITY 1:
Carousel Activity:
- Write the following words on flip chart paper and post them on the classroom walls: Punishment, Revenge, Reconciliation, and Retribution.
- Ask the students to write their "first thoughts" about each word.
- After they have completed responding to each word, ask the students to write one word or statement under the appropriate word.
- Break students into four groups and distribute one word per group. Have each group discuss and present the collective thinking about the word they were given.
- As a class, discuss the responses and decide which approach will bring about the best resolution.

ACTIVITY 2:
Give students the following quotations and discuss their meanings:

"Until we can forgive, we will never be free."
–Nelson Mandela (anti-apartheid activist, former President of South Africa)

"If you want to make peace with your enemy, you have to work with your enemy. Then he becomes your partner."
–Nelson Mandela

"Reconciliation is to understand both sides; to go to one side and describe the suffering being endured by the other side, and then go to the other side and endure the suffering being endured by the first side."
–Thich Nhat Hanh (Vietnamese monk and activist)

- Divide students into two groups for a debate. Allow time for students to discuss their strategies for the debate and to write talking points.
- One side should argue that reconciliation is necessary.
- One side should argue against reconciliation.
- After the debate, discuss how neither side of the debate has to exclude the other.
- Reconciliation includes justice.
- Use this quote:

"Reconciliation should be accompanied by justice, otherwise it will not last. While we all hope for peace, it shouldn't be peace at any cost but peace based on principle, on justice."
–Corazon Aquino (former President of the Philippines; first female president in Asia)

- Point out continuing problems in countries or for groups which have not reconciled.
- Have students try to think of other countries in which reconciliation has succeeded or failed.
- Students should pick a divided country/region and write a paragraph of forgiveness from the perspective of each side to the other.

INTERNATIONAL HUMAN RIGHTS FRAMEWORK

Since the creation of the Universal Declaration of Human Rights (UDHR) by the United Nations (UN) in 1948, many other international documents have been drafted to develop these rights further. These documents include other declarations and resolutions, as well as treaties—which are also called covenants or conventions. Countries commit to protect the rights recognized in these documents. Sometimes a specific institution is created within the UN to monitor countries' compliance.

Here are examples of relevant international documents:

- Convention on the Elimination of Racial Discrimination (CERD)
  - **Article 3** Prevention, Prohibition, and Eradication of Apartheid and Racial Segregation
  - **Article 5** Elimination of Racial Discrimination
  - **Article 6** Protection and Remedies against Racial Discrimination
- International Covenant on Civil and Political Rights (ICCPR)
- International Covenant on Economic, Social and Cultural Rights (ICESCR)

For more information, visit the Office of the High Commissioner for Human Rights' website:
www.ohchr.org

BECOME A DEFENDER

Watch the video clip "Desmond Tutu: Hope in Troubled Times": **www.youtube.com/watch?v=ILCdwJj37iw.** While Archbishop Tutu is widely known for his role in the Truth and Reconciliation hearings in South Africa, he is a passionate believer that each and every person can make a difference.

- Start a peer mediation program in your school. If there is already one, become involved.
- Create materials such as posters and brochures to use in a teach-in at your school, community center, faith-based group, or civic group. The materials should specify a global conflict (including the U.S.) and attempts to reconcile the parties' differences. Consider how these local groups could assist in helping the global organizations.
- Draft a play using a global conflict that is in negotiations for reconciliation. Use information from the Archbishop's interview and videos, as well as knowledge of social studies to write a convincing argument for reconciliation.

ADDITIONAL RESOURCES

CONFLICT TRANSFORMATION AND RECONCILIATION IN RWANDA:
www.peacemakers.ca/research/Africa/RwandaPeaceLinks.html
This website lists organizations working on peacebuilding in Rwanda. This list consists of both government and civil society organizations and is largely edited by its readership.

THE CENTRE FOR THE STUDY OF VIOLENCE AND RECONCILIATION:
www.csvr.org.za
The mission of the CSVR is to understand and prevent violence, heal its effects and build sustainable peace at community, national and regional levels through collaboration with and learning from the lived and diverse experiences of communities affected by violence and conflict.

THE FELLOWSHIP OF RECONCILIATION:
forusa.org/
The Fellowship of Reconciliation, with a history of almost a hundred years of work for peace, justice and non-violence, focuses the power of compassionate action by individuals throughout the world to their work for reconciliation.

EURASIANET.ORG:
www.eurasianet.org/
EurasiaNet.org provides information and analysis about political, economic, environmental and social developments in the countries of Central Asia and the Caucasus, as well as in Russia, Turkey, and Southwest Asia.

THE INTERNATIONAL INSTITUTE FOR DEMOCRACY AND ELECTORAL ASSISTANCE:
www.idea.int/conflict/sr/
The International Institute for Democracy and Electoral Assistance (International IDEA) focuses on supporting stronger democratic institutions and processes, and more sustainable, effective and legitimate democracy.

"FORGIVENESS DOESN'T MEAN PRETENDING THINGS AREN'T AS THEY REALLY ARE. FORGIVENESS IS THE RECOGNITION THAT A GHASTLINESS HAS HAPPENED. AND FORGIVENESS DOESN'T MEAN TRYING TO PAPER OVER THE CRACKS, WHICH IS WHAT PEOPLE DO WHEN THEY SAY, 'LET BYGONES BE BYGONES.' BECAUSE THEY WILL NOT. THEY HAVE AN INCREDIBLE CAPACITY FOR ALWAYS RETURNING TO HAUNT YOU." —Archbishop Desmond Tutu

ROBERT F. KENNEDY
United States — Justice

Robert Francis Kennedy was born on Nov. 20, 1925, in Brookline, Mass., the seventh child of Rose and Joseph P. Kennedy. After high school, he served in the Navy during World War II, attended Harvard University and later the University of Virginia Law School. In 1950, Robert Kennedy married Ethel Skakel and later had 11 children. In 1952, Kennedy managed his older brother John's successful campaign for the U.S. Senate from Massachusetts. Later, he worked in the U.S. Senate, winning attention as the Senate's lead lawyer investigating Teamsters' Union leader Jimmy Hoffa for corruption. In 1960, he managed John F. Kennedy's presidential campaign and was appointed Attorney General in President Kennedy's cabinet after the election where he won respect for his effective administration of the Department of Justice. Robert Kennedy also helped President Kennedy propose the most far-reaching civil rights law since Reconstruction, the Civil Rights Act of 1964, which passed eight months after President Kennedy's death.

Soon after President Kennedy's death, Robert Kennedy resigned as Attorney General and, in 1964, ran successfully for the United States Senate in New York. On March 18, 1968, Robert Kennedy announced his candidacy for the Democratic presidential nomination. He challenged the complacent in American society and sought to bridge the great divides in American life—between the races, between the poor and the affluent, between young and old.

Robert Francis Kennedy was fatally shot on June 5, 1968, at the Ambassador Hotel in Los Angeles, Calif., shortly after claiming victory in that state's crucial Democratic primary. He was 42 years old.

Robert F. Kennedy was committed to the principles of freedom and social justice and carried a message of hope and an unflagging conviction that courage would bring change.

EXCERPT FROM RFK'S "DAY OF AFFIRMATION" SPEECH GIVEN AT THE UNIVERSITY OF CAPE TOWN, SOUTH AFRICA, JUNE 6TH, 1966

"EVERY TIME WE TURN OUR HEADS THE OTHER WAY WHEN WE SEE THE LAW FLOUTED; WHEN WE TOLERATE WHAT WE KNOW TO BE WRONG; WHEN WE CLOSE OUR EYES AND EARS TO THE CORRUPT BECAUSE WE ARE TOO BUSY, OR TOO FRIGHTENED; WHEN WE FAIL TO SPEAK UP AND SPEAK OUT—WE STRIKE A BLOW AGAINST FREEDOM AND DECENCY AND JUSTICE." —Robert F. Kennedy

Our answer is the world's hope; it is to rely on youth. The cruelties and obstacles of this swiftly changing planet will not yield to obsolete dogmas and outworn slogans. It cannot be moved by those who cling to a present which is already dying, who prefer the illusion of security to the excitement and danger which comes with even the most peaceful progress.

This world demands the qualities of youth; not a time of life but a state of mind, a temper of the will, a quality of the imagination, a predominance of courage over timidity, of the appetite for adventure over the love of ease. It is a revolutionary world we live in, and thus, as I have said in Latin America and Asia, in Europe and in the United States, it is young people who must take the lead. Thus you, and your young compatriots everywhere, have had thrust upon you a greater burden of responsibility than any generation that has ever lived.

"There is," said an Italian philosopher, "nothing more difficult to take in hand, more perilous to conduct, or more uncertain in its success than to take the lead in the introduction of a new order of things." Yet this is the measure of the task of your generation, and the road is strewn with many dangers. First, is the danger of futility: the belief there is nothing one man or one woman can do against the enormous array of the world's ills—against misery and ignorance, injustice and violence. Yet many of the world's greatest movements, of thought and action, have flowed from the work of a single man. A young monk began the Protestant Reformation, a young general extended an empire from Macedonia to the borders of the earth, and a young woman reclaimed the territory of France. It was a young Italian explorer who discovered the New World, and the thirty-two-year-old Thomas Jefferson who proclaimed that all men are created equal.

"Give me a place to stand," said Archimedes, "and I will move the world." These men moved the world, and so can we all. Few will have the greatness to bend history itself, but each of us can work to change a small portion of events, and in the total of all those acts will be written the history of this generation. Thousands of Peace Corps volunteers are making a difference in isolated villages and city slums in dozens of countries. Thousands of unknown men and women in Europe resisted the occupation of the Nazis and many died, but all added to the ultimate strength and freedom of their countries. It is from numberless diverse acts of courage and belief that human history is shaped. Each time a man stands up for an ideal, or acts to improve the lot of others, or strikes out against injustice, he sends forth a tiny ripple of hope, and crossing each other from a million different centers of energy and daring those ripples build a current which can sweep down the mightiest walls of oppression and resistance.

"If Athens shall appear great to you," said Pericles, "consider then that her glories were purchased by valiant men, and by men who learned their duty." That is the source of all greatness in all societies, and it is the key to progress in our time.

The second danger is that of expediency; of those who say that hopes and beliefs must bend before immediate necessities. Of course, if we would act effectively we must deal with the world as it is. We must get things done. But if there was one thing President Kennedy stood for that touched the most profound feelings of young people around the world, it was the belief that idealism, high aspirations, and deep convictions are not incompatible with the most practical and efficient of programs—that there is no basic inconsistency between ideals and realistic possibilities, no separation between the deepest desires of heart and of mind and the rational application of human effort to human problems. It is not realistic or hardheaded to solve problems and take action unguided by ultimate moral aims and values, although we all know some who claim that it is so. In my judgment, it is thoughtless folly. For it ignores the realities of human faith and of passion and of belief—forces ultimately more powerful than all of the calculations of our economists or of our generals. Of course to adhere to standards, to idealism, to vision in the face of immediate dangers takes great courage and takes selfconfidence. But we also know that only those who dare to fail greatly, can ever achieve greatly.

It is this new idealism which is also, I believe, the common heritage of a generation which has learned that while efficiency can lead to the camps at Auschwitz, or the streets of Budapest, only the ideals of humanity and love can climb the hills of the Acropolis.

A third danger is timidity. Few men are willing to brave the disapproval of their fellows, the censure of their colleagues, the wrath of their society. Moral courage is a rarer commodity than bravery in battle or great intelligence. Yet it is the one essential, vital quality of those who seek to change a world which yields most painfully to change. Aristotle tells us that "At the Olympic games it is not the finest and the strongest men who are crowned, but they who enter the lists… So too in the life of the honorable and the good it is they who act rightly who win the prize." I believe that in this generation those with the courage to enter the moral conflict will find themselves with companions in every corner of the world.

For the fortunate among us, the fourth danger is comfort, the temptation to follow the easy and familiar paths of personal ambition and financial success so grandly spread before those who have the privilege of education. But that is not the road history has marked out for us. There is a Chinese curse which says "May he live in interesting times." Like it or not, we live in interesting times. They are times of danger and uncertainty, but they are also more open to the creative energy of men than any other time in history. And everyone here will ultimately be judged—will ultimately judge himself—on the effort he has contributed to building a new world society, and the extent to which his ideals and goals have shaped that effort.

So we part, I to my country and you to remain. We are—if a man of forty can claim that privilege—fellow members of the world's largest younger generation. Each of us have our own work to do. I know at times you must feel very alone with your problems and difficulties. But I want to say how impressed I am with what you stand for and the effort you are making; and I say this not just for myself, but for men and women everywhere. And I hope you will often take heart from the knowledge that you are joined with fellow young people in every land, they struggling with their problems and you with yours, but all joined in a common purpose; that, like the young people of my own country and of every country I have visited, you are all in many ways more closely united to the brothers of your time than to the older generations of any of these nations; and that you are determined to build a better future. President Kennedy was speaking to the young people of America, but beyond them to young people everywhere, when he said that "the energy, the faith, the devotion which we bring to this endeavor will light our country and all who serve it—and the glow from that fire can truly light the world."

And he added, "With a good conscience our only sure reward, with history the final judge of our deeds, let us go forth to lead the land we love, asking His blessing and His help, but knowing that here on earth God's work must truly be our own."

COURAGEOUS IDEAS, WORDS AND ACTIONS FOR HUMAN RIGHTS FOR ALL
ROBERT F. KENNEDY

LESSON GRADE LEVEL: 9–12
HUMAN RIGHTS ISSUES: POVERTY, VOTING RIGHTS, JUSTICE, EDUCATION, EQUAL ACCESS

UNIVERSAL DECLARATION OF HUMAN RIGHTS:
Full Spectrum

GUIDING QUESTIONS:
- What human rights did Robert F. Kennedy defend?
- How did Robert F. Kennedy work to advance human rights?
- How do words and speeches inform and inspire action?

TIME REQUIREMENT:
225 Minutes (Five 45-minute lessons)

OBJECTIVES:
By the end of the lesson, students will:
- Understand the power of words and speeches to inform and inspire people.
- Identify different ways to defend human rights using the speeches and work of Robert F. Kennedy.
- Assess the breadth and scope of human rights issues during RFK's life and what the status of those human rights are today.

COMMON CORE LEARNING STANDARDS:
- CCSS.ELA-LITERACY.RI.9-10.1
- CCSS.ELA-LITERACY.RI.9-10.2
- CCSS.ELA-LITERACY.RI.9-10.3
- CCSS.ELA-LITERACY.RI.9-10.4
- CCSS.ELA-LITERACY.RI.9-10.5
- CCSS.ELA-LITERACY.RI.9-10.6
- CCSS.ELA-LITERACY.RI.9-10.7
- CCSS.ELA-LITERACY.RI.9-10.8
- CCSS.ELA-LITERACY.RI.9-10.9
- CCSS.ELA-LITERACY.RI.9-10.10

STUDENT SKILLS
- Public Speaking
- Analyzing
- Presentation Planning
- Reflecting
- Drawing Conclusions

TECHNOLOGY REQUIRED:
- Access to the Internet
- Projection system for film clips and PowerPoints

MATERIALS:
- Universal Declaration of Human Rights:
  www.un.org/en/documents/udhr
- Robert F. Kennedy quotes:
  www.rfkhumanrights.org/robert-f-kennedy

NOTE TO TEACHERS
For further and more in-depth analysis on the issues addressed in this lesson, please have your students visit
www.rfkhumanrights.org/robert-f-kennedy/robert-f-kennedy-legacy-education-project

STUDENT ACTIVITIES

ANTICIPATORY SET:
- Have students review the Universal Declaration of Human Rights (UDHR).
- In pairs, ask students to review quotes by Robert F. Kennedy: www.rfkhumanrights.org/robert-f-kennedy. The students should focus on the Ripple of Hope Speech as well as speeches that address the following topics: poverty, justice and civil rights.
- Have the students align articles of the UDHR with RFK quotes

ACTIVITY 1:
- Put students in groups of 4
- Ask each group to select 1 RFK quote to focus on for this project.
- Have each group research the full speech and respond to the following questions:
    - Where did RFK give the speech?
    - What was the occasion for the speech?
    - Who was the audience?
    - What was his main message? If more than one, please identify the additional messages.
    - Review the original list of articles from the UDHR that aligned with this speech. Are other articles applicable?
- Ask the group to prepare a class presentation.

ACTIVITY 2:
- In the same group, now ask the students to research the issues addressed in the RFK speech in today's context.
    - How has the issue changed? Has it?
    - How is the issue being addressed?

CULMINATING ACTIVITY
- Have each group write a speech addressing one or more of the issues RFK addressed in the speech they researched.
- Each member of the group will read a part of the speech to the whole class.

INTERNATIONAL HUMAN RIGHTS FRAMEWORK

Since the creation of the Universal Declaration of Human Rights (UDHR) by the United Nations (UN) in 1948, many other international documents have been drafted to develop these rights further. These documents include other declarations and resolutions, as well as treaties—which are also called covenants or conventions. Countries commit to protect the rights recognized in these documents. Sometimes a specific institution is created within the UN to monitor countries' compliance.

Here are examples of relevant international documents:

- UN General Assembly Declaration on Human Rights Defenders
    - **Article 1:** Right to promote and to seek protection of human rights
    - **Article 2:** Responsibility of governments to protect, promote, and implement all human rights
    - **Article 5:** Right to assemble peacefully, form non-governmental organizations, and conduct human rights work individually and in association with others
    - **Article 8:** Right to make complaints about government policies concerning human rights and to have the complaints reviewed
    - **Article 9:** Right to benefit from an effective remedy in case these rights are violated
    - **Article 11:** Right to the lawful occupation or profession of a human rights defender
- International Covenant on Civil and Political Rights (ICCPR)
- International Covenant on Economic, Social and Cultural Rights (ICESCR)

For more information, visit the Office of the High Commissioner for Human Rights' website:
www.ohchr.org

BECOME A DEFENDER

Students will carry out a school and community wide education and advocacy project. Based on what the students learned about the life and work of Robert F. Kennedy, they will design and carry out an education and advocacy campaign. The goals of the campaign should include:

1 **RAISE AWARENESS:**
Make the student body and community aware of how the issues they researched are still a concern today. Students may create posters, fliers, host speakers, table at area markets.

2 **TAKE ACTION:**
Host a "drive" at their school to assist community members in need; write a letter to their representative requesting attention to a local matter related to poverty, justice or civil rights; volunteer with an organization working to address issues of poverty, justice or civil rights.Collect and use student questions to facilitate the group discussion Make questions from ALL readings. Include South Africa and Chicago in the questioning.

ADDITIONAL RESOURCES

ROBERT F. KENNEDY HUMAN RIGHTS:
www.rfkhumanrights.org
Learn more about the life and vision of Robert F. Kennedy.

NYSUT SPEAK UP, SPEAK OUT CURRICULUM:
www.nysut.org/resources/all-listing/2008/october/speak-up-speak-out-rfk-social-justice-curriculum
New York State United Teachers curriculum and resource materials designed to help instill in students the concept of social justice and the principles of a just society, using the legacy of Robert F. Kennedy.

RFK LEGACY EDUCATION:
www.rfkhumanrights.org/robert-f-kennedy/robert-f-kennedy-legacy-education-project
An online, educational resource examining the life, work and words of Robert F. Kennedy

MAKE GENTLE THE LIFE OF THE WORLD: THE VISION OF ROBERT F. KENNEDY:
Kennedy, Robert F. *Make Gentle the Life of the World: The Vision of Robert F. Kennedy*. Harcourt, 1998.
Highlights of RFK's personal journal, which features favorite quotations of great thinkers throughout history, along with moving portions of Robert Kennedy's most memorable speeches.

THIRTEEN DAYS: A MEMOIR OF THE CUBAN MISSILE CRISIS:
Kennedy, Robert F. *Thirteen days: A memoir of the Cuban missile crisis*. WW Norton & Company, 2011.
A behind-the-scenes account of the thirteen days in October 1962, when the United States confronted the Soviet Union over its installation of missiles in Cuba.

ROBERT KENNEDY AND HIS TIMES:
Schlesinger, Arthur M. *Robert Kennedy and his times*. Houghton Mifflin Harcourt, 2012.
Insight into RFK's private papers, letters, and journals, providing a fresh perspective of his personal relationships and public events, written by a close friend of Robert F. Kennedy.

"ALL GREAT QUESTIONS MUST BE RAISED BY GREAT VOICES, AND THE GREATEST VOICE IS THE VOICE OF THE PEOPLE—SPEAKING OUT—IN PROSE, OR PAINTING OR POETRY OR MUSIC, SPEAKING OUT—IN HOMES AND HALLS, STREETS AND FARMS, COURTS AND CAFÉS—LET THAT VOICE SPEAK AND THE STILLNESS YOU HEAR WILL BE THE GRATITUDE OF MANKIND."

—Robert F. Kennedy

RIGOBERTA MENCHÚ TUM
Guatemala – Indigenous People's Rights

Rigoberta Menchú Tum is a heroine to Maya Indians in Guatemala and indigenous peoples throughout the world. Born into an impoverished family in 1959, the daughter of an active member of the CUC (Committee of Campesinos [Agricultural Workers]), she joined the union in 1979, despite the fact that several members of her family had been persecuted for their membership. In the early 1980s, the Guatemalan military launched a "scorched earth campaign," burning over four hundred Maya villages to the ground, massacring hundreds of children, women, and the infirm; and brutally torturing and murdering anyone suspected of dissenting from the policy of repression. The military killed up to two hundred thousand people, mostly Maya Indians, and forced one million people into exile. Menchú's mother and brother were kidnapped and killed, and her father burned alive. While the Guatemalan army marched against its people, the rest of the world remained almost completely silent. In 1983, Menchú published her autobiography, an account of the Guatemalan conflict. *I, Rigoberta Menchú* was translated into twelve languages, and was an influential factor in changing world opinion about support for the Guatemalan military. Fifteen years later, discrepancies were found about certain details of the work, but there is no dispute regarding its essential truth and the massive suffering of Guatemala's indigenous peoples at the hands of the hemisphere's most brutal military government. In 1992, Rigoberta Menchú Tum won the Nobel Peace Prize for her work. Menchú has been forced into exile three times for her advocacy within Guatemala, and despite the threats, she continues her work today on human rights, indigenous rights, women's rights, and development. In 1993 she was named as a UNESCO Goodwill Ambassador. She has been active in trying to attain justice for the Guatemalan genocide, even pursuing claims today in Spanish courts, due to the legacy of impunity in her home country.

INTERVIEW TAKEN FROM KERRY KENNEDY'S BOOK *SPEAK TRUTH TO POWER*, 2000

"I WAS A MILITANT WOMAN IN THE CAUSE OF JUSTICE. AND FOR TWELVE YEARS I DID NOT HAVE A HOME OF MY OWN OR A FAMILY." —Rigoberta Menchú Tum

Struggles for the rights of poor people, for dignity, for human life, seem to be very, very dark tunnels, but one should always try, in that struggle, to find some light and some hope. The most important thing to have is a great quantity of positive feelings and thoughts. Even though one can easily be pessimistic, I always attempt to look for the highest values that human beings could possibly have. We have to invent hope all over again. One day, sadly, I said to myself with great conviction: the death of my parents can never be recuperated. Their lives cannot be brought back. And what can also never, never be recuperated is the violation of their dignity as human beings. Nothing will ever convince me that anything could happen to pay back that debt.

Now, I don't think this realization is a personal matter; rather, it is a social question. It's a question of a society, of history, of all memory. Those of us who are victims are the ones that decide what pardons are going to take place, and under what sort of conditions. We, who have survived the crimes, are the ones who should have the last words, not those observing. I respect the opinions of those who say that a decree or an accord or a religious philosophy is enough to pardon others, but I really would like, much more than that, to hear the voice of the victims. And at this moment, the victims are really not listened to.

An amnesty is invented by two actors in a war. It's hardly the idea of the victims, or of the society. Two armed groups who have been combating each other decide that it is best for each to pardon the other. This is the whole vulgar reality that the struggle for human rights has to go through at this moment.

An agreement with real dialogue would bring war to an end as soon as possible. But I never could accept that two sides that have committed horrendous atrocities could simply pardon themselves. What the amnesties do is simply forget and obliterate, with one simple signature, all the violations of human rights that have taken place. Many of these abuses continue in the lives of the victims, in the orphans of that conflict. So even though there are amnesties in countries such as Argentina, Chile, El Salvador, and Guatemala, I can see that people do not forget the human rights violations that they have suffered, and they continue to live with them. These are things that are not going to be forgotten.

A real reconciliation has to be based on the search for truth. We who are the victims of these abuses have a right to the truth. Finding the truth is not enough. What we also have to find is justice. And the ways, the processes, and the means by which this justice can be accomplished are through law and through the courts, through procedures that are legal.

This is why I now have a legal case in Guatemala against the military. We have a lot of corrupt judges, we know about bribery and threats. The military does not want to set a precedent for real justice, so they bribe the entire legal system. One of these days that system will become more fair. But we have to give time to the system of justice to improve.

Living in a country of such violence, of such a history of blood, no one, no one would want to bring a child into this world. I was a militant woman in the cause of justice. And for twelve years I did not have a home of my own or a family. I lived in refugee camps when I could. I lived in the homes of nuns in Mexico. I left behind many, many bags in many different countries, in many different buildings. Under those circumstances, what would I have done with a child? I was involved in all kinds of risks, and thought that maybe I would have to sacrifice my life for my people. When one says that, you understand, it is not just a slogan, but a real-life experience. I exposed myself to the most difficult kinds of situations.

For me stability began with a wish: it was very important to find, once again, my sister Ana. She was the youngest of the family. She had decided that she was going to live with me, but I didn't have a home where she could live. I began to actually have the desire to have a home, a desire that coincided with the time when I was awarded the Nobel Peace Prize. Many friends, people who gave me counseling, thought that it would be better for me, too. After all, you can't have a Nobel Prize winner wandering around the world semi-clandestinely!

I give thanks to Mexico—to the people of Mexico, and at that time, to the authorities, the officials of Mexico City—who offered me that sense of stability in a very short period of time. The Office of the Mayor gave me a house, and in that house we were able to construct for ourselves, once again, a very normal life. We were once again a family. I'd left Guatemala in 1981, but though I'd returned in 1988, I was detained, so I was forced to leave again. After that I would come and go in and out of Guatemala, but I could never stay for very long. Finally, in 1994, we went back, officially.

Home is important to me for another reason. I have two children now—one who I lost. It just changes around your life completely when you have a child, doesn't it? You can't be just moving around the world in any way that you want anymore. So you live life according to the circumstances that you are in. I can't say, though, that I ever had the intention of living my life, or any part of my life, quite the way in which I lived it! Things just happened. Suddenly I was caught up in the situation. And I tried to overcome it, with a lot of good will and not a whole lot of introspection. Now my son lives with my family, with my sister and my nephews; there are seven children in the house. There are two twins, two years old, a daughter of my sister-in-law, and four children who don't have a father. But we live in a large family, and that gives my son a great deal of satisfaction. He has a community every day.

My youngest son, whose name was Tzunun, which means hummingbird, was part of a very, very difficult pregnancy. It was risky from the very first day. It required a tremendous desire to be a mother, to carry it through, and I had decided to have this child. All my work, all my activities had to be stopped. Still, so sadly, he lived only three days. But when he died I thought that he had lived with me for many, many years. I talked to him, I understood him, we thought he could perceive things around him.

During this time, I was always thinking about the world and listening to the news and trying to find out what was going on. And when you really listen it has a very, very big impact on you. Because when you are going around to conferences and talking to people and people are applauding you, you really don't fully realize what a terrible situation that women and children are in. But being at home, in your own four walls, and knowing what is happening in the world, you really feel very limited in what you are doing and what you can do. My child gave me time to sit back and to think about the condition of women, and children who don't have parents, and children who are abused by their parents. My situation, my condition as a mother is a great, great privilege: not just some kind of decree, or law, or desire, but something that, fundamentally, has transformed my life.

There have been a lot of successes in my life. And when you have success, it helps you to want to continue the struggle. You are not alone, for it's not true that it is only pain that motivates people to continue struggling to make their convictions a reality. The love of many other people, the support that one has from other people, and above all, the understanding of other people, has a lot to do with it. It's when one realizes that there are a lot of other people in the world that think the way you do, that you feel you are engaged in a larger undertaking. Every night when I go to sleep, I say a prayer that more people, more allies will support the world's struggles. That's the most important thing. That would be so good.

INDIGENOUS PEOPLES' RIGHTS
RIGOBERTA MENCHÚ TUM

LESSON GRADE LEVEL: 9–12
HUMAN RIGHTS ISSUES: LEGAL PROTECTION; DISCRIMINATION; TORTURE; GENOCIDE; PROPERTY; FREE EXPRESSION

UNIVERSAL DECLARATION OF HUMAN RIGHTS:

Article 1: Right to Equality
Article 3: Right to Life, Liberty, and Personal Security
Article 7: Right to Equality before the Law
Article 9: Freedom from Arbitrary Arrest and Exile
Article 15: Right to a Nationality and the Freedom to Change It
Article 17; Right to Own Property
Article 19: Freedom of Opinion and Information

TIME REQUIREMENT:
205 Minutes

GUIDING QUESTIONS:
- What are the rights and responsibilities of citizens in a democracy?
- What factors influence people's perspectives?
- What were the key events in Rigoberta Menchú's experiences?
- How were human rights violated in Guatemala?
- How did Rigoberta Menchú's Nobel Prize affect the world's view of the incidents in Guatemala?

OBJECTIVES:
After this lesson, students will be able to:
- Describe the key events in Rigoberta Menchú's experiences.
- Analyze the causes and effects of the decisions Rigoberta Menchú made as she became a defender.
- Explain the meaning of specific human rights and provide examples of human rights violations in Guatemala in the 1980s.
- Explain what it means to be an indigenous person.
- Evaluate text and write critiques from two perspectives.

MATERIALS:
- Copies of newspaper article for activity 3 www.argentinaindependent.com/tag/spanish-embassy/
- Menchú's Nobel Acceptance Speech: www.nobelprize.org/nobel_prizes/peace/ laureates/1992/
- Copies of the UDHR: www.un.org/en/ documents/udhr/

COMMON CORE LEARNING STANDARDS:
- CCSS.ELA-LITERACY.RH.11-12.1
- CCSS.ELA-LITERACY.RH.11-12.3
- CCSS.ELA-LITERACY.RH.11-12.8

VOCABULARY:
- Indigenous
- Discrimination
- Marginalized
- Repression
- Oppression
- Condemned
- Exile
- Inhospitable
- Emancipation
- Embassy
- Red Cross
- Amnesty International

CONCEPTS:
- Human Rights
- Social Justice
- Power in Society

TECHNOLOGY REQUIRED:
- Internet
- LCD projector to show video clip

STUDENT ACTIVITIES

ANTICIPATORY SET:
Students will briefly respond to prompts in their notebooks:
- Describe a time you or someone close to you has been a victim of unfair treatment.
- What are three words to describe how this experience made you feel?
- How did you respond to this treatment? (e.g., yell, fight, talk with a friend or adult, stay quiet)

ACTIVITY 1:
- Watch a video clip of film trailer for *When the Mountains Tremble* (available on TeacherTube and YouTube). This clip briefly introduces a situation in Guatemala when thousands of people were victims of unfair treatment and how Rigoberta Menchú chose to respond.
- Students will read the biography of Rigoberta Menchú Tum (www.peacejam.org/nobels/rigoberta-mench%C3%BA) and answer the six questions below:
    o What were the major events in Rigoberta Menchú's early life?
    o How do you think these experiences made her feel?
    o What did these feelings motivate her to do? How did she stand up to violence and injustice?
    o What was she putting at risk when she made these choices?
    o What did she accomplish with her choices?
    o What were the negative consequences of her choices?
- Class discussion and debriefing about questions 1-6 and their personal connections from the warm up.
- Students write their responses to questions 7 and 8, in class or as homework.
    o What would motivate you to take the kinds of risks and suffer the negative consequences she did? Choose one situation that would affect you or someone close to you and choose one issue that would affect a bigger group of people whom you aren't personally connected to.
    o In light of your personal reflection, what type of person do you think Rigoberta Menchú Tum is? What is most important for someone to know about her?

ACTIVITY 2:
- Students will respond to the following question: What rights do you think all people deserve?
- The teacher will divide the class into small groups.
- Students will work with their small group to read quotations from Rigoberta Menchú Tum's Nobel acceptance speech, match them with UDHRs, and write explanations of how each quotation represents a universal human right or a violation of a universal human right.
- The teacher will lead a class discussion about the groups' explanations of quotations and human rights.

ACTIVITY 3:
- Students will read an American newspaper account of a peasant protest in Guatemala City in 1980. www.argentinaindependent.com/currentaffairs/latest-news/newsfromlatinamerica/guatemala-spanish-embassy-massacre-trial-begins
- Students will write a critique of this article from two perspectives.
    o How do you think a Guatemalan Maya peasant, like Rigoberta Menchú Tum, would respond to this newspaper account of the 1980 peasants' protests? What would he or she think is most and least accurate about the article? Write at least one sentence that this person would want to add to the article.
    o How do you think a Guatemalan government official, like the President or an army General, would respond to this newspaper account of the 1980 peasant protests? What would he or she think is most and least accurate about the article? Write at least one sentence that this person would want to add to the article.
- Teacher will lead a class discussion in which students share the responses they wrote.

CULMINATING ACTIVITY:
- Students will create a collage representing the basic human rights addressed in this lesson.
- After completing their collage, students will write a response to the following question:
    o Based on the images you chose for your collage, why was a government able to violate these basic human rights?

INTERNATIONAL HUMAN RIGHTS FRAMEWORK

Since the creation of the Universal Declaration of Human Rights (UDHR) by the United Nations (UN) in 1948, many other international documents have been drafted to develop these rights further. These documents include other declarations and resolutions, as well as treaties—which are also called covenants or conventions. Countries commit to protect the rights recognized in these documents. Sometimes a specific institution is created within the UN to monitor countries' compliance.

Here are examples of relevant international documents:

- International Covenant on Civil and Political Rights (ICCPR)
    - **Article 2** Right to Be Free from Discrimination
    - **Article 7** Prohibition of Torture or Cruel, Inhuman, or Degrading Treatment or Punishment
    - **Article 14** Right to Equality before the Courts and Tribunals and to a Fair Trial
    - **Article 19** Right to Freedom of Expression and Opinion
- Convention against Torture and Other Cruel, Inhuman and Degrading Treatment or Punishment (CAT)
- International Convention on the Elimination of All Forms of Racial Discrimination (CERD)

For more information, visit the Office of the High Commissioner for Human Rights' website:
www.ohchr.org

BECOME A DEFENDER

Students will design and carry out a campaign to make the student body aware of issues that may affect their peers. Students may create fliers, posters, buttons, etc. Topics may include the following:
- Homelessness
- Poverty
- Undocumented individuals
- Bullying
- Abuse (mental and physical)

After researching the issues that affect their local community, students may participate in the following activities:
- Volunteer in a homeless shelter
- Create a "drive" at their school for clothing, food, toiletries, or school supplies for the homeless

EXPANDING OPPORTUNITIES
- Find a local defender: Explore their community and find an organization or individual who is a defender for their community. Students will interview these individuals for an oral history and nominate their "defender" for a Nobel Peace Prize.
- Students will identify a conflict happening around the world. They will analyze the role and the potential leverage the U.S. government (and/or corporations) plays in the conflict. Students will conduct an awareness campaign about the conflict (e.g., write letters, make phone calls, etc.) to U.S. Congressional leaders.
- The DREAM Act enables children of undocumented parents to be eligible for scholarship funding. Students will research and learn about the DREAM Act, educate their peers about provisions of the DREAM Act, and participate in an advocacy campaign to build support for national legislation.

ADDITIONAL RESOURCES

PEACE JAM:
www.peacejam.org

Peace Jam is an organization that brings young people together with Nobel Peace Laureates to tackle challenging issues facing the planet. Peace Jam addresses a broad range of issues, from basic needs, such as access to water, to basic rights, such as human security. Peace Jam online provides a short bio of Rigoberta Menchú Tum's early life and achievements, as well as a video interview of Tum and the Global Call to Action.

ABOUT.COM:
Latinamericanhistory.about.com

About.com is divided into topic sites, which are grouped into channels and cover diverse subjects and issues. The content is written by a network of writers, referred to as Guides, who have experience in the subjects they write about. latinamericanhistory.about.com/od/historyofcentralamerica/p/menchu.htm provides a brief bio of Rigoberta Menchú Tum's life and continuing legacy.

AMERICAN INDIAN HERITAGE FOUNDATION:
www.indians.org/welker/menchu2.htm

This website is ideal for searching and reading the bibliographies and foundations of many leaders and defenders of American Indian communities.

RIGOBERTA'S HUMAN FORUM SPEECH:
www.youtube.com/watch?v=yvnUEup1hC4

1992 Nobel Peace Prize winner Rigoberta Menchú Tum discusses her inspiring life as well as the human condition at The Human Forum Conference. Check out www.anhglobal.org for more information. Part One of Two.

"A VOICE FOR INDIGENOUS PEOPLE":
www.youtube.com/watch?v=daM0NiBBnwc

Rigoberta Menchú Tum is a Nobel Peace Prize laureate, indigenous woman and survivor of genocide in Guatemala. She seeks the observance of a code of ethics for an era of peace as her contribution to humanity. This YouTube video gives a brief overview of issues facing the indigenous population in Guatemala and provides a solid contextual basis for understanding the importance of Tum's work.

HISTORICAL CLARIFICATION COMMISSION:
www.aaas.org/sites/default/files/migrate/uploads/mos_en.pdf

The Historical Clarification Commission, ordered in 1994 by the Oslo Accords, investigated the numerous human rights violations committed during the Civil War period in Central America. The final report, though substantial (in length as well as content), provides a solid context for the work of Rigoberta Menchú Tum.

MARKKULA CENTRE FOR APPLIED ETHICS:
www.scu.edu/ethics

The Markkula Center for Applied Ethics supports individuals and organizations to make better choices that care for others and protect our shared environment.

VAN JONES
United States – Law Enforcement

Van Jones is the Founding Director of the Ella Baker Center for Human Rights. Established in 1996 and named for an unsung civil rights heroine, the Center challenges human rights abuses in the U.S. criminal justice system. A project of the Ella Baker Center, Bay Area Police Watch, is committed to stopping police misconduct and protecting victims of abuse. Jones's efforts to establish civilian oversight, and to require transparency and accountability within disciplinary proceedings, have yielded results. Jones's efforts to ban the use of pepper spray, routinely used by police in subduing suspects, has helped launch a nationwide campaign against the chemical weapon. The Police Watch Hotline documents callers' complaints and refers victims to lawyers who are, in turn, trained by Police Watch in handling misconduct cases. Police Watch then helps victims and lawyers through legal proceedings, organizes community support, and advocates on behalf of victims to public officials and the media. Jones is the author of *The Green Collar Economy,* the definitive book on "green jobs." In 2008—thanks to a low-cost, viral marketing campaign—his book became an instant New York Times bestseller. Jones helped to pass America's first "green job training" legislation, the Green Jobs Act, which George W. Bush signed into law as a part of the 2007 Energy Bill. He is the recipient of many awards and honors, including the Reebok International Human Rights Award; the World Economic Forum's Young Global Leader designation; and the prestigious, international Ashoka Fellowship. *TIME* magazine named him an environmental hero in 2008. In 2009, *TIME* named him one of the 100 most influential people in the world. From March to September 2009, Jones worked as the special adviser for green jobs at the White House Council for Environmental Quality. He is currently a political correspondent on CNN, and is the founder and President of Rebuild the Dream.

INTERVIEW TAKEN FROM KERRY KENNEDY'S BOOK *SPEAK TRUTH TO POWER*, 2000

> "A GUY IS BEATEN, HE'S KICKED, HE'S STOMPED, HE'S PEPPER-SPRAYED, GAGGED (BECAUSE THE POLICE DIDN'T WANT HIM BLEEDING ON THEM), AND THEN LEFT IN A CELL. WELL, THAT'S THE SORT OF STUFF YOU EXPECT IN GUATEMALA, BUT IT HAPPENED JUST FIFTEEN OR TWENTY MINUTES FROM HERE." —Van Jones

The Ella Baker Center for Human Rights is a strategy center for documenting and exposing human rights violations in the United States—particularly those perpetuated by law enforcement. A project of the Center, Bay Area Police Watch, has a hotline that opened in 1995 here in the San Francisco Bay area and in 1998 in New York City where people can call and report abuses. We designed a computer database, the first of its kind in the country, that allows us to track problem officers, problem precincts, problem practices, so at the click of a mouse we can now identify trouble spots and troublemakers. This has given us a tremendous advantage in trying to understand the scope and scale of the problem. Now, obviously, just because somebody calls and says, "Officer so-and-so did something to me," doesn't mean it actually happened, but if you get two, four, six phone calls about the same officer, then you begin to see a pattern. It gives you a chance to try and take affirmative steps.

We also try to expose abuse by doing a lot of public education. This is something we've really pioneered. Sometimes when people who suffered abuse at the hands of the police tried to engage the mainstream media, they would do it in a way that made them seem shrill, alarmist, or racially divisive. Instead, we thought it was important to interact intelligently with the media in a way that let them know that we were credible and interested in moving this issue forward in a responsible way.

Look, we get ten phone calls a day here from survivors of police misconduct and violence. Some of it is, "Officer so-and-so called me a boogerhead," or something minor like that, but it also goes as far as wrongful death. We see the full gamut here. We try to spend half an hour to an hour with every person who calls. We have people who call because their children have come home with a broken arm or broken jaw or their teeth shattered or because the child has been held in jail for four or five days with no charges. What we do when people call is that we let them tell their story and then we write the story into the computer. We don't try to rush them.

Then we tell them about their rights and their remedies. We tell them if you want to file a complaint with this officer in this municipality, here's the number you call, here's how to get the form to fill out, here's the process. We tell them if you want to bring a lawsuit or file a claim of some sort for money damages, here's what that process looks like.

If a caller has evidence of police brutality, then we have a couple dozen cooperating attorneys that we refer those cases to. Those attorneys rely on us to screen to a certain extent—to ask enough questions about the incidents so that if somebody calls and says, "Police Watch told me to call," then they can be relatively confident that there's at least something to work with here.

We started out in January 1995 at the Lawyers' Committee for Civil Rights. Even though police issues were not a part of their docket (they usually focus on employment, discrimination, and other issues), they saw a need.

That need became clear, after we had been doing this project for a while, in the Aaron Williams case. This was the African-American man who died in police custody. We had a really close relationship to the process. Sometimes you have to have a certain amount of professional distance, but this case was not like that at all. Here the family and Police Watch volunteers merged efforts and spent those two years literally arm-in-arm. We went through three separate disciplinary hearings for the same officer on the same case within eight months, and we lost the first two times and we finally won in 1997. I'll never forget the look on the officer's face. It had gone beyond Aaron. This case became a question of not letting the authorities get away with this level of wholesale disrespect and disregard for human life and for the rule of law. Community witnesses, several dozen of them, all said that after Aaron was down on the ground and handcuffed, the policeman was kicking him in the head with cowboy boots, and that he was identifiable because he was the only officer in plainclothes.

Aaron had been sprayed in the face with pepper-spray, which is not a gas, like mace—it's a resin. The resin sticks to your skin and it burns and it continues to burn until it's washed off. The police never washed the resin off Aaron. And so this guy is beaten, he's kicked, he's stomped, he's pepper-sprayed, gagged (because they didn't want him bleeding on them), and then left in a cell. Well, that's the sort of stuff you expect in Guatemala, but it happened just fifteen or twenty minutes from here.

All of this was illegal and inhumane and yet it was going to be sloughed under the rug. This case was definitely a turning point in my life. I knew what kind of officer this was; I knew what the family was going through and I just made a commitment inside myself that I was not going to walk away. Win or lose, this family was not going to fight by itself. Every resource that I had, every bit of creativity that I had, all of the training in criminal law and community organizing that I had, I was going to put to work until we got justice.

As a result, I began to get threats. "Who do you think is protecting you?" or if something were to happen to you, talking about "People like you don't deserve to live"; "People like you don't deserve to be in this city." It just went on and on.

But 99 percent of the cases don't end as dramatically as Williams's. We have this one African-American father who bought a sports car for his son. On the boy's sixteenth birthday, he was driving him home in this new sports car and the police pulled him over—two black guys in a sports car. Now they put them on the hood of the car, they frisked them, they went all through the car. There was no physical violence but the guy wound up with a severe emotional and nervous breakdown. His small business went under. He just couldn't recover from it because he was so humiliated in front of his son.

My point is that this sort of stuff just shouldn't be happening. It doesn't make our world any safer, doesn't make law enforcement's job any easier. It increases the level of resentment against law enforcement. And it's plain just wrong.

"WHO DO YOU THINK IS PROTECTING YOU?"
VAN JONES

LESSON GRADE LEVEL: 9–12, AND HIGHER EDUCATION
HUMAN RIGHTS ISSUES: JUSTICE, FAIR TREATMENT

UNIVERSAL DECLARATION OF HUMAN RIGHTS:
Article 3: Right to Life, Liberty and Personal Security
Article 5: Freedom from Torture and Degrading Treatment
Article 6: Right to Recognition as a Person before the Law
Article 7: Right to Equality before the Law
Article 9: Freedom from Arbitrary Arrest and Exile

GUIDING QUESTIONS:
- What role does law enforcement play in society?
- What responsibility does the media, in its many forms, have to the larger society?
- What mechanisms or institutions are in place to provide oversight of law enforcement agencies?
- What can we learn about real priorities by reviewing approved budgets?

TIME REQUIREMENT:
120 minutes

OBJECTIVES:
After this lesson, students will:
- Know who Van Jones is and why he is a human rights defender.
- Understand the issue of excessive force used by police within the U.S. and internationally.
- Understand the impact media has in advancing a position or perspective on an issue.
- Understand the connection between policies and financing policy positions.
- Examine the roles of oppression, repression, and police brutality.

COMMON CORE LEARNING STANDARDS:
- CCSS.ELA-LITERACY.RH.9-10.1
- CCSS.ELA-LITERACY.RH.9-10.2
- CCSS.ELA-LITERACY.RH.9-10.4
- CCSS.ELA-LITERACY.WHST.9-10.7
- CCSS.ELA-LITERACY.WHST.9-10.9
- CCSS.ELA-LITERACY.RH.11-12.1
- CCSS.ELA-LITERACY.RH.11-12.2
- CCSS.ELA-LITERACY.WHST.11-12.7
- CCSS.ELA-LITERACY.WHST.11-12.9

VOCABULARY:
- Inhumane
- Impunity
- Intimidation
- Racial profiling
- Misconduct
- Brutality

CONCEPTS:
- Justice
- Civil rights
- Human rights
- Equal protection
- Police misconduct
- Racial profiling

TECHNOLOGY REQUIRED:
Internet access

MATERIALS:
- Interview with Van Jones from *Speak Truth To Power* www.rfkhumanrights.org / click on Speak Truth To Power / click on "Curricula" link
- *Lessons from a Killing* by Van Jones brasscheck.com/cm/jones.html

STUDENT ACTIVITIES

Note to Teachers: Discuss with students the difficulties of being a police officer to better understand the officer's perspective. The role of an officer needs to be presented before the issue of police brutality is discussed.

ANTICIPATORY SET:

- Instruct students to read the Van Jones interview from *Speak Truth To Power* and to read the article *Lessons from a Killing*.
- Ask students to respond to the following questions:
  - What is excessive force? Is there a base standard or is it situational?
  - The Aaron Williams case happened 15 years ago. Do you think the situation has changed? Explain.
  - Identify three strategies regarding work with the media that Van Jones implemented in order to achieve justice for Aaron Williams.
  - Did Van Jones believe all police to be racist?

ACTIVITY 1:

Have the students analyze vocabulary related to the issue of policing and use of force. Ask students to:

- Define the term;
- Identify if the term is used in U.S. and/or international law;
- Is the term biased and if so, towards whom? Is the bias implicit and if so, is the bias one-directional?

Reasonable force • Excessive use of force
Justified use of force • Police misconduct
Police brutality • Use of force incident

ACTIVITY 2:

Split the class into two groups. One group will be given a case of excessive use of force by police in the U.S. and the other group will be given an international case. (If time permits, have students research and then select the case they will work on.) Ask the students to examine the following four aspects of the case:

- How was the case covered by the media? Be sure to review at least two print media sources and at least three online sources. Ask students to highlight key differences in reporting the case. Did they find explicit bias? Towards which party?
- Identify the primary and secondary players in the case. Did the case stay within the established law enforcement and judicial systems? Did community organizations get involved?
- What was the police response to the alleged abuse? What was their rationale for the level of force used in the situation?
- What legal framework did the prosecution and defense use to try their cases? Did they reference state, provincial, national, federal and/or international law? Which ones?
- How was the case resolved? What was the response of primary and secondary players? What impact did the decision have on the ability of police to do their job? Did the outcome of the case generate more interest or coverage than the initial case? If so, how?

ACTIVITY 3:

- Have each group present its findings to the class.
- On the board or interactive whiteboard note the similarities and differences between how the U.S. and the international cases were handled.
- Have the class discuss the joint findings guided by the following questions:
  - Was justice served? Explain.
  - What could have been done differently by:
    Defense • Prosecution • Community Support Groups • Media • Law Enforcement
- Have the class draw final conclusions about the prevalence of excessive use of force by police and how it should be addressed.
- Their conclusion should lead to an action plan to bring the issue of policing and community to some public forum.

ACTIVITY 4:

Frame the class for students by explaining the connection between campaign promises or statements made to the media, advancing and passing policies, and advancing and passing a budget to fully support policy implementation.

- Ask students to select a state, making sure that there is geographic diversity.
- Have students research their selected state's budget.

Specifically, have students focus on the following budget lines: **Education • Law Enforcement • Justice System • Prison System • Social Services**
- After the budget analysis, have the students write a paper addressing trends between the interface with communities where money is and is not spent and law enforcement and the criminal justice system.
- Ask students to draw their own conclusion as to the effect of bias in our society as it impacts communities both from a budget allocation and law enforcement perspective. Ask students to include suggested policy changes to address human rights violations that their research uncovers.

INTERNATIONAL HUMAN RIGHTS FRAMEWORK

Since the creation of the Universal Declaration of Human Rights (UDHR) by the United Nations (UN) in 1948, many other international documents have been drafted to develop these rights further. These documents include other declarations and resolutions, as well as treaties—which are also called covenants or conventions. Countries commit to protect the rights recognized in these documents. Sometimes a specific institution is created within the UN to monitor countries' compliance.

Here are examples of relevant international documents:

- International Covenant on Civil and Political Rights (ICCPR)
    - **Article 6:** Right to life
    - **Article 9:** Right to liberty and security of person, including the right to freedom from arbitrary arrest or detention
- Convention Against Torture and Other Cruel, Inhuman and Degrading Treatment or Punishment (CAT)
    - **Article 1:** Definition of torture as severe pain or suffering, whether physical or mental, intentionally inflicted upon a person by a public official to obtain information, punish the person, intimidate the person, or for any reason based upon discrimination of any kind
    - **Article 10:** Requirement that law enforcement personnel, such as police officers, are trained on the prohibition against torture and other cruel, inhuman, and degrading treatment
- International Convention on the Elimination of All Forms of Racial Discrimination (ICERD)
    - **Article 5:** Right to equality before the law, notably in relation to the right to personal security and the right to protection against violence or bodily harm, whether inflicted by government officials or private individuals
- United Nations Basic Principles on the Use of Force and Firearms by Law Enforcement Officials
- United Nations Code of Conduct for Law Enforcement Officials

For more information, visit the Office of the High Commissioner for Human Rights' website: **www.ohchr.org**

BECOME A DEFENDER

- While it is important to trust what is in the news, it is much more difficult to discover what is truly going on. Interview known victims, friends and family of victims, and the police force to hear the official accounts and what is not being reported by the government or media.
- Invite members of local law enforcement agencies—local police, county sheriffs, state police—to your class to talk about what the job of being a police officer entails and what training officers have to prevent excessive use of force.
- Discuss and debate your and your classmates' perceptions of police brutality compared with what is in the law, what is portrayed in the media, and by the government. Do they align with each other? Compile stories of local, national and international police brutality and argue the pros and cons of the case. Do you believe that the amount of force was merited?
- If there has been a specific instance of excessive use of force by police in your area, prepare materials for a teach-in at your school to inform students and teachers about police brutality and how to work with the local police force to end it. This information can also be shared with civic and community organizations.
- Research the United States' official position on the excessive use of force by police. What actions does the U.S. Department of Justice take against law enforcement agencies that violate U.S. laws on excessive use of force?
- Research United States Supreme Court decisions on cases dealing with excessive use of force by police. Create a timeline of cases and their outcomes. Prepare a report for your class on the cases and outcomes.
- Contact organizations within the United States that work to hold police accountable and build community relations with law enforcement. Find out what you can do to help and organize a branch of that organization locally.
- Write to a federal official and file a complaint if you believe that what you have seen, heard, read, or experienced is a form of excessive use by police.
- Find out what the state of excessive use of force by police is in other nations, whether they are democracies, dictatorships, conflict zones, or peace-keeping nations. Countries must work together to reduce excessive force by law enforcement worldwide. Prepare materials to present to your class and civic and community organizations on the background of these abuses and what actions can be taken to end such activities in these countries.
- Write to the United Nations Human Rights Council citing reasons to end global abuses of law enforcement.
- Research international organizations dedicated to ending police brutality and volunteer to work on their cause.

> "THIS CASE BECAME A QUESTION OF NOT LETTING THE AUTHORITIES GET AWAY WITH THIS LEVEL OF WHOLESALE DISRESPECT AND DISREGARD FOR HUMAN LIFE AND FOR THE RULE OF LAW." –Van Jones

ADDITIONAL RESOURCES

VAN JONES WEBSITE:
www.vanjones.net
A website dedicated to the initiatives of Van Jones that includes resources for students and volunteers to get involved.

ELLA BAKER CENTER FOR HUMAN RIGHTS:
www.ellabakercenter.org
The Ella Baker Center for Human Rights provides a number of opportunities for activism both through local and national programs.

UNITED NATIONS HOME PAGE:
www.un.org/en

COMMUNITIES UNITED AGAINST POLICE BRUTALITY:
www.cuapb.org/
A non-profit organization that works to enact legislative change to prevent police brutality and support the victims of police brutality in Minnesota.

POLICE CRIMES:
PoliceCrimes.com
This website dedicated to raising awareness of cases of police brutality provides a forum for the discussion of crimes committed by police officers, as well as police ethics fact sheets.

"PICKETS, RIOTS & POLICE BEATINGS— THE 2004 REPUBLICAN NATIONAL CONVENTION IN NEW YORK CITY:"
www.vimeo.com/7104734
An hour-long documentary on police repression and brutality from the 2004 protests during the RNC in New York.

STOP POLICE BRUTALITY:
www.policebrutality.info
Website detailing the latest police brutality cases, including articles, photos, videos and more.

DETROIT COALITION AGAINST POLICE BRUTALITY:
www.detroitcoalition.org/about
A non-profit organized to help prevent police brutality by strengthening the communities of Detroit.

STOP AND FRISK REPORT:
ccrjustice.org/stop-and-frisk-human-impact
This report documents some of the stories behind the staggering statistics behind aggressive stop-and-frisk practices, and sheds new light on the breadth of impact this policy is having onindividuals and groups, in neighborhoods, and citywide.

REBUILD THE DREAM:
www.rebuildthedream.com
Founded by Van Jones, Rebuild the Dream is a grassroots movement that works to transform the core values and beliefs of the American people to ultimately bring about political and social change.

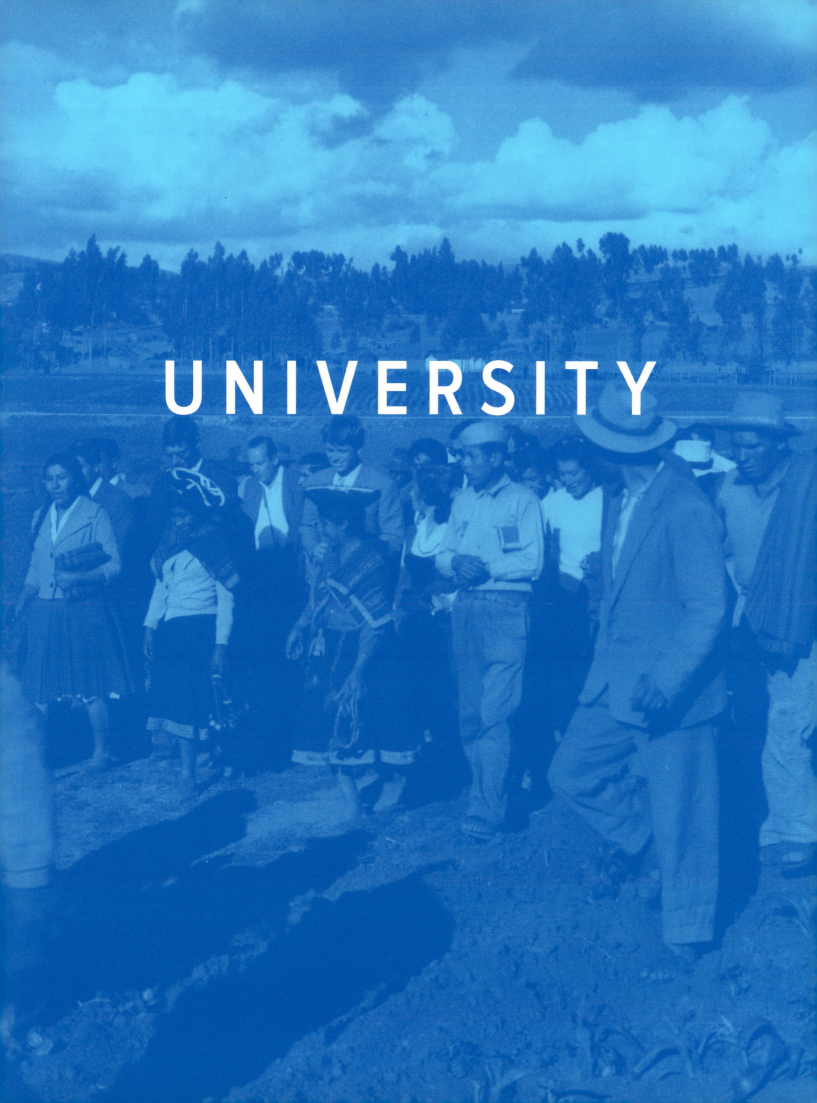
UNIVERSITY

MARINA PISKLAKOVA
Russia – Domestic Violence

Marina Pisklakova is Russia's leading women's rights activist. She studied aeronautical engineering in Moscow, and while conducting research at the Russian Academy of Sciences, was startled to discover that family violence had reached epidemic proportions. Because of her efforts, Russian officials started tracking domestic abuse and estimate that, in a single year, close to 15,000 women were killed and 50,000 were hospitalized, while only one-third to one-fifth of all battered women received medical assistance. With no legislation outlawing the abuse, there were no enforcement mechanisms, support groups, or protective agencies for victims. In July 1993, Pisklakova founded a hotline for women in distress, later expanding her work to establish the first women's crisis center in the country. She lobbied for legislation banning abuse, and worked with an openly hostile law enforcement establishment to bring aid to victims and prosecution to criminals. She began a media campaign to expose the violence against women and to educate women about their rights, and regularly appears on radio and television promoting respect for women's rights. Today her organization ANNA (also known as the National Center for the Prevention of Violence) operates a network of 170 crisis centers across Russia and the former Soviet Union. She is now active not only in combating the scourge of violence against women, but also in the trafficking of women and children. In 2004, she received the Human Rights Global Leadership Award. Pisklakova's efforts have saved countless lives, at great risk to her own.

INTERVIEW TAKEN FROM KERRY KENNEDY'S BOOK *SPEAK TRUTH TO POWER*, 2000

"THE OFFICER SEEMED NICE, BUT THEN HE IMMEDIATELY CALLED THE HUSBAND AND SAID TO HIM, "WHAT IS YOUR WIFE DOING? AND WHY IS SHE GOING AROUND TALKING ABOUT FAMILY MATTERS? LOOK, IF YOU DO IT, DO IT QUIETLY." I REALIZED HOW HOPELESS THE PROBLEM REALLY WAS FOR HER. "–Marina Pisklakova

When I started the first domestic violence hotline in Russia in 1993 (we named it ANNA, Association No to Violence), I was alone, answering calls four hours a day, every day, for six months. I was counseling people in person the other four hours. I couldn't say no; there were so many women. I had no training, no distance, no boundaries. But at the same time, I don't know how I could have done anything differently.

Without realizing what I was embarking upon, I began this work while a researcher at the Institute for Socio-Economic Studies of the Population within the Russian Academy of Sciences. While coordinating a national survey on women's issues, one day I received a survey response I did not know how to classify. It described a woman's pain and suffering at the hands of her husband. I showed it to some colleagues and one of them told me, "You have just read a case of domestic violence." I had never heard this term before. It was not something even recognized in our post-Soviet society, much less discussed. I decided I needed to learn more about this mysterious phenomenon.

Shortly thereafter, I encountered the mother of one of my son's classmates in front of the school. Half of her face was severely bruised. She wouldn't tell me what had happened. One evening a few days later, she called me. Her story shocked me. When her husband was wearing a suit and the button fell off, and it was not fixed quickly, he took a shoe and slapped his wife in the face. For two weeks she couldn't go out. She was really distressed, and hurt—physically and emotionally hurt—because half her face was black and blue. I asked her, "Why don't you just leave him?" A very typical question. And she said, "Where would I go?" I said, "Divorce him. Get another apartment." She said, "I depend on him completely." And in this exchange, I saw everything: the way the abuser was consolidating control, decreasing self-confidence, and diminishing self-esteem. I also heard her story of how he would come home and go to the kitchen, touch the floor with his finger, and, if there was the slightest dirt, ask sneeringly, "What did you do all day?" The floors in Russian kitchens always have some dirt, especially if you have kids at home who are running around—the kitchen is often the center of family life in our small apartments. For outsiders, scenes such as I have just described might seem ridiculous, but I was to soon discover that they were commonplace. For this woman, our conversation was an opportunity to communicate with someone who didn't judge her, who didn't say, "What did you do wrong?" I didn't realize that I had actually started counseling her. But I did realize from her story that from psychological violence comes physical violence.

So I started thinking that I should help her; I should refer her to somebody. And then I realized that there was nowhere to go. I cannot tell you my feelings. I really felt hopeless and helpless. In Russia there is a saying, "He beats you, that means he loves you." I now knew the meaning of that saying. I asked myself, "What can you do about a cultural attitude?" But I knew what I had to do. I started the hotline. One cold January day, a woman called in and I started talking with her. After a few minutes, she stopped, saying, "I am not going to talk to you on the phone. I need to see you." So I said, "Okay," and when she came in, her first tearful words were, "I'm afraid my husband is going to kill me and nobody will know." She told me her story. Her husband was very nice until she told him she was pregnant. At that point, everything turned upside down. He became very controlling. She was vulnerable and dependent: "I was terrified; his face was not happy. It was like he'd won. As though he was thinking, 'It's my turn. Now I can do whatever I want to you.'" The danger was real.

My first reaction was, "Oh, my God, what am I going to do now?" I knew the police would do nothing. But I called the police in her district anyway. The officer seemed nice, but then he immediately called the husband and said to him, "What is your wife doing? And why is she going around talking about family matters? Look, if you do it, do it quietly." I realized how hopeless the problem really was for her. Her problem became mine. I could not walk away. I called a woman I knew who was a retired lawyer and said, "I don't have any money and this woman doesn't have any money. But she needs help. She needs a divorce and a place to live." In Moscow, housing is a big problem. When this woman married her husband, she traded her apartment to his family and now his brother lived there. So she had nowhere to go. She was trapped. Her story got worse. When their first baby was nine months old, her husband tried to kill her. "I don't know how I survived," she told me. The lawyer and I helped her file for divorce. That's when the husband told her, "I will kill you and nobody will know. And I will just say to everybody that you ran off with another man and left your baby." I started calling her every morning just to make sure that she was alive. For three months, the lawyer counseled us at each stage and helped us develop a plan.

In the midst of all of this, the situation took a scary turn. The woman called and said: "They know everything we are talking about!" Her mother-in-law worked at the phone company and we quickly figured out that she was listening to her calls. I said, "You know, maybe it's better. Let them hear about all the support that you have outside." So we started pretending we had done more than we actually had. On the next phone call, I started saying, "Okay, so this police officer is not helpful, but there are lots of other police I am going to talk to about it and your lawyer will, too. So don't worry." The next time she came to see me, and she said, "They became much more careful after we started talking that way." Eventually her husband left their apartment, partly because the lawyer told us how to get him out, and partly because he and his family realized that she was educated about her rights now. Ultimately, they got a divorce. Her father-in-law came to see her and said, "You have won, take the divorce, and take back the apartment; you will never see my son again."

Soon after this success, a friend of hers in a similar situation started legal proceedings against her own ex-husband and also got her apartment back. I was elated, and for the first time, encouraged! Even in Russian society, where there were few legal precedents, a woman who is willing to do so can stand up for her rights and win. But these stories are just a small fraction of the thousands we continue to hear day after day. Unfortunately, most of the women who call us do not know their rights, nor do they know that they do not have to accept the unacceptable.

There have been some bad moments along the way. One time I picked up the phone and a male voice started saying, "What is this number?" I was cautious since it was not common for a man to call our hotline like that. I responded with "Well, what number did you dial?" And he said, "I found this phone number in the notes of my wife and I am just checking—what is it?" I told him, "Why don't you ask your wife? Why are you calling?" And at first he tried to be calm and polite, saying, "Look, I'd just like you to tell me what it is." And I said, "If you don't trust your wife, it's your problem. I am not going to tell you what it is and I am not asking your name. If you introduce yourself maybe we can talk." And then he started being really aggressive and verbally abusive and he said, "I know who you are. I know your name. I know where you are located. I know where you live. And I am going to come there with some guys and kill you." My husband was there with me at the time and saw I was really scared, though I said to the man on the phone, "I am not afraid of you," and just hung up. I still don't know whose husband it was. He never came. Another time, my phone at home rang late at night and a man said, "If you don't stop, you'd better watch out for your son." This really scared me. I moved my son to my parents' home for a few months. That was tough for a mother to do.

There are different estimations of domestic violence in Russia. Some say now that 30 to 40 percent of families have experienced it. In 1995, in the aftermath of the Beijing Women's Conference, the first reliable statistics were published in Russia indicating that 14,500 women a year had been killed by their husbands. But even today, the police do not keep such statistics, yet their official estimates are that perhaps 12,000 women per year are killed in Russia from domestic violence. Some recognition of the dimensions of this problem is finally surfacing.

Under Russian law, however, only domestic violence that results either in injuries causing the person to be out of work for at least two years, or in murder, can be considered a crime. There are no other laws addressing domestic violence in spite of years of effort to have such laws enacted by the Duma. But, in my work and in our fledgling women's movement, we have on our own expanded the functional definition of domestic violence to include marital rape, sexual violence in the marriage or partnership, psychological violence, isolation, and economic control. This latter area has become perhaps one of the most insidious and hidden forms of domestic violence because women comprise 60 percent of the unemployed population—and the salary of a woman is about 60 percent of a man's for the same work.

A friend started working with me in January 1994, and by that summer we had trained our first group of women who began to work with us as telephone counselors. In 1995, I started going to other cities in Russia, putting on training sessions for other women's groups that were starting to emerge and who wanted to start hotlines or crisis centers. Next, we started developing programs to provide psychological and legal counseling for the victims of domestic violence.

By 1997, we had also started a new program to train lawyers in how to handle domestic abuse cases. Under present Russian law, the provocation of violence is a defense which can be argued in court to decrease punishment. This is perhaps the most cruel form of psychological abuse, because it all happens in the courtroom right in front of the victim. She is made to look responsible. The victim is blamed openly by the perpetrator. Regrettably, there are still many judges who will readily accept the notion that she was in some way responsible, and let the perpetrator avoid being held accountable for his actions. The final trauma has been inflicted.

At the start of the new millennium, we have over forty women's crisis centers operating throughout Russia, and have recently formed the Russian Association of Women's Crisis Centers, which is officially registered with and recognized by the Russian government. I am honored to have been elected as its first President.

My parents have been incredibly supportive of my work. My father, a retired military officer, once said to me, "In Soviet times you would have been a dissident, right?" And my reply to him was, "Probably, because the Soviets maintained the myth of the ideal—where domestic violence couldn't exist, officially." The attitude during Soviet times was that if you are a battered wife, then you had failed as a woman and as a wife. It was the woman's responsibility in our society to create a family atmosphere. It was up to her to maintain the ideal. That's why women came to me who had been brutalized for twenty-six years. I was the first person they could turn to openly, and confide something they had to hide within themselves throughout their life. This is still true to a great extent today.

I am not an extraordinary person. Any woman in my position would do the same. I feel, however, that I am really lucky because I was at the beginning of something new, a great development in Russia, a new attitude. Now, everybody is talking about domestic violence. And many are doing something about it.

VIOLENCE AGAINST WOMEN
MARINA PISKLAKOVA

HUMAN RIGHTS ISSUES: WOMEN'S RIGHTS, FREEDOM FROM VIOLENCE, INDIVIDUAL INTEGRITY

UNIVERSAL DECLARATION OF HUMAN RIGHTS:
- **Article 3:** Right to Life, Liberty, and Personal Security
- **Article 5:** Freedom from Torture and Degrading Treatment

TIME REQUIREMENT:
80 minutes

TEACHER TIP:
Domestic violence is a difficult subject to address because it is often hidden and is often a cause of shame for the victim and those close to the victim. In preparing to teach this subject, make sure to have available the names and contact details of community programs that support individuals affected by domestic violence. It is also important to explain what domestic violence is: any of a series of behaviors used by one person in a relationship to control the other. Partners may be married or not married; heterosexual, gay, or lesbian; living together, separated or dating.

WHAT KINDS OF BEHAVIORS CAN BE CONSIDERED DOMESTIC VIOLENCE?
If your partner:
- Intentionally insults or embarrasses you
- Controls any of your actions, including who you see or talk to or where you go
- Tells you that you are a bad parent or threatens to take away or hurt your children
- Makes all of your decisions for you
- Prevents you from seeing loved ones, like your friends and family
- Physically assaults you in any way
- Takes your possessions or money and withholds it from you
- Intimidates you with weapons
- Destroys your possessions or threatens to kill your pets
- Attempts to scare you
- Threatens to do physical harm to themselves or to you
- Prevents you from going to work or school

GUIDING QUESTIONS:
- What does it mean to be safe?
- Where does one expect to be safe?
- Why did the authors of the Universal Declaration of Human Rights use the language "Personal Security"?
- Where does domestic violence occur?

OBJECTIVES:
After this lesson students will be able to:
- Define and understand the term "gender-based violence."
- Examine and analyze the facts and figures related to domestic violence.
- Know who Marina Pisklakova is and the critical importance of her work for survivors of violence.

VOCABULARY:
- Gender-based violence
- Personal security
- Domestic violence
- Prevention
- Relationship
- Dissident

CONCEPTS:
- Empathy
- Identity
- Justice
- Power
- Decision-making
- Civic values
- Human rights

TECHNOLOGY REQUIRED:
- Internet access

MATERIALS:
- Universal Declaration of Human Rights
  www.un.org/en/documents/udhr/index.shtml
- Domestic Violence www.domesticviolence.org
- Domestic violence facts and figures
  www.ncadv.org/learn/statistics

STUDENT ACTIVITIES

ANTICIPATORY SET:
- Instruct students to read Article 3 of the Universal Declaration of Human Rights.
- Instruct students to read the definition of domestic violence and the facts and figures.
- After reading, instruct students to rephrase Article 3 based on their understanding of domestic violence.
- Ask students to report orally to class via teacher-facilitated discussion.

ACTIVITY 1:
- Distribute to the class the interview with Marina Pisklakova. www.rfkhumanrights.org / click on Speak Truth To Power / click on "Curricula" link
- Ask students the following questions:
  - Why did Marina Pisklakova begin her work to end domestic violence in Russia?
  - What are some characteristics of domestic violence that are similar from case to case?
  - What is Pisklakova's functioning definition of domestic violence?
  - What is a dissident? Why would Pisklakova's father call her a dissident?
  - Describe how Pisklakova has helped Russian women.

ACTIVITY 2:
- Conduct a community mapping exercise to learn about where a survivor of domestic violence can get help and support in your community. Include health care providers, law enforcement, community non-profits, and the justice system.
- After the mapping project is complete, pair students off and have them select one organization to interview.
- Prior to conducting the interview, the class, as a whole, should develop at least 10 questions to ask each organization. A common set of questions will enable the class to create a report on the community's capacity to assist victims of domestic violence.
- Once the interviews are complete, students should work in groups of four to review their interview responses and draft a common document.
- After the groups have met, convene the full class to draft one document outlining the similar and different ways in which community organization fulfills its mission to assist victims of domestic violence.
- Students may share this document with the organizations.
- As a result of this activity students could develop an action plan to change some aspect of their community safety net, or an acknowledgement to their city or town for doing a good job.

BECOME A DEFENDER

- Host a Personal Safety Day. Include speakers and presenters from some of the community organizations you learned about in your community mapping exercise. Make available a self-defense class.
- Invite a speaker to address the issue of dating violence.
- Set up a table at a popular neighborhood site and provide information about domestic violence, organizations working to stop it, and opportunities for individuals to take action.
- Have a petition-signing in support of both U.S. and International laws to protect women and to stop violence against women and girls.

INTERNATIONAL HUMAN RIGHTS FRAMEWORK

Since the creation of the Universal Declaration of Human Rights (UDHR) by the United Nations (UN) in 1948, many other international documents have been drafted to develop these rights further. These documents include other declarations and resolutions, as well as treaties—which are also called covenants or conventions. Countries commit to protect the rights recognized in these documents. Sometimes a specific institution is created within the UN to monitor countries' compliance.

Here are examples of relevant international documents:

- International Covenant on Civil and Political Rights (ICCPR)
  - **Article 3:** Equal rights for men and women
  - **Article 6:** Right to life and to not be arbitrarily deprived of it
  - **Article 7:** Right to be free from torture and Cruel, Inhuman or degrading treatment (CIDT)
  - **Article 17:** Protection of privacy and from unlawful attacks on honor and reputation
- International Covenant on Economic, Social and Cultural Rights
- Convention Against Torture and Other Cruel, Inhuman or Degrading Treatment or Punishment
- Convention on the Elimination of All Forms of Discrimination Against Women

For more information, visit the Office of the High Commissioner for Human Rights' website:
www.ohchr.org

ADDITIONAL RESOURCES

WHO WORLD HEALTH ORGANIZATION:
www.who.int
WHO publishes periodic reports on gender discrimination and domestic violence. This site is a good source for statistics and other health and development information.

UN WOMEN:
www.unwomen.org/en
UN Women features information about gender equality and women's empowerment on an international level.

UNFPA UNITED NATIONS POPULATION FUND:
www.unfpa.org/public/
The UNFPA is an international development agency that works to promote every individual's right to health and equal opportunities. It focuses on population data to develop policies and programs that reduce poverty and promote overall health and well-being.

NATIONAL COALITION AGAINST DOMESTIC VIOLENCE:
www.ncadv.org/
NCADV is an American-based non-profit that organizes women and their allies to end violence against women and children on a national level by addressing perpetuating conditions that condone this kind of violence.

UNICEF REPORT ON DOMESTIC VIOLENCE:
www.unicef-irc.org/publications/pdf/digest6e.pdf
This report from UNICEF covers domestic violence from numerous angles. It addresses the current scope and magnitude through statistics, while also examining the causes and consequences. The UNICEF report also addresses the obligations of the state and suggests strategies and interventions.

NATIONAL DOMESTIC VIOLENCE HOTLINE:
www.thehotline.org
A website built around the National Domestic Violence Hotline that raises awareness of domestic violence and provides services to victims, survivors and their families.

THE DALAI LAMA
Tibet – Religious Freedom

The ninth child born to a farming family in the Chinese border region of Amdo in 1935, two-year-old Lhamo Thondup was recognized by Tibetan monks as the fourteenth reincarnation of the Dalai Lama, considered a manifestation of the Bodhisattva of Compassion. Renamed Tenzin Gyatso, he was brought to Lhasa to begin a sixteen-year education in metaphysical and religious texts to prepare him for his role as spiritual leader. The Chinese invasion of Tibet in 1949, and its aftermath, introduced brutal repressions in which thousands of Tibetans were executed in prisons or starved to death in prison camps, and hundreds of monasteries, temples, and other cultural and historic buildings were pillaged and demolished. In their effort to eradicate Tibetan culture and identity, the Chinese forced Tibetans to dress like Chinese, to profess atheism, to burn books, and to condemn, humiliate, and kill their elders and teachers. His life in jeopardy, the Dalai Lama fled into exile in northern India along with 80,000 Tibetans in 1959; he has never returned. Meanwhile, new waves of repression erupted in the 1960s and 1980s that continue in the present. To date, the Chinese government has murdered, massacred, tortured, or starved to death more than one million Tibetans, one-fifth of the population. In the face of this state oppression, where do Tibetans gather strength to continue the struggle? His Holiness the Dalai Lama inspires Tibetans to embrace their beliefs and hold fast to their dreams. He has demanded that we think of those who have stolen his land and massacred his people, not as murderers and thieves, but as human beings deserving of forgiveness and compassion. Since 1959, His Holiness has received more than 84 awards, honorary doctorates, and other prizes, including the Nobel Peace Prize in 1989, in recognition of his lifelong message of peace, non-violence, inter-religious understanding, universal responsibility, and compassion. His Holiness has also authored more than 72 books and describes himself as a simple Buddhist monk.

INTERVIEW TAKEN FROM KERRY KENNEDY'S BOOK *SPEAK TRUTH TO POWER*, 2000

"UNLESS THE WORLD COMMUNITY TACKLES THE TIBETAN ISSUE, THE HUMAN RIGHTS VIOLATION WILL CONTINUE."–The Dalai Lama

ON COMPASSION

When I visited the Nazi death camps of Auschwitz, I found myself completely unprepared for the deep revulsion I experienced at the sight of the ovens where hundreds of thousands of human beings were burned. The sheer calculation and detachment to which they bore horrifying witness overcame me. This is what happens, I thought, when societies lose touch with feeling. And while it is necessary to have legislation and international conventions in place to prevent such disasters, these atrocities happen in spite of them. What of Stalin and his pogroms? What of Pol Pot, architect of the Killing Fields? And what of Mao, a man I knew and once admired, and the barbarous insanity of the Cultural Revolution? All three had a vision, a goal, with some social agenda, but nothing could justify the human suffering engendered. So, you see it all starts with the individual, with asking what the consequences are of your actions. An ethical act is a nonharming act. And if we could enhance our sensitivity to others' suffering, the less we would tolerate seeing others' pain, and the more we would do to ensure that no action of ours ever causes harm. In Tibetan we call this *nying je*, translated generally as compassion.

ON SUFFERING

All human beings desire happiness, and genuine happiness is characterized by peace. A sentient being experiences suffering as well. It is that experience that connects us to others and is the basis of our capacity for empathy. Many in Tibet have experienced the suffering of having what we want taken away from us. As refugees, we have lost our country, and have been forcibly separated from our loved ones. When I hear bad news from Tibet my natural reaction is one of great sadness. By the late seventies and early eighties there was an influx of large numbers of Tibetans who came to see me in India and spoke about how their fathers or their parents or their brothers or sisters were killed and how they themselves had been tortured or suffered. I often wept. Now, after hearing so many cases, my eyes have become dry. It's like the soldier who is scared when he hears the first shot, but after many shots becomes familiar with the sound.

And when the Chinese lost their temper with me, and they took it out on the Panchen Lama, that was very sad, and I accept some responsibility for what happened. Yet, what could I do? When these things occur there is no point in being discouraged and sad. Feelings of helpless anger do nothing but poison the mind, embitter the heart, and enfeeble the will. I take comfort in the words of the ancient Indian master Shantideva's advice, "If there is a way to overcome the suffering, then there is no need to worry. If there is no way to overcome the suffering, then there is no use in worrying." We must place this in context and remind ourselves that the basic human disposition toward freedom, truth, and justice will eventually prevail. It is also worth remembering that the time of greatest difficulty is the time of greatest gain in wisdom and strength. A great Tibetan scholar who spent more than twenty years in prison enduring terrible treatment, including torture, wrote letters during his confinement and smuggled them out—and they were acclaimed by many as containing the most profound teachings on love and compassion ever heard.

ON ETHICS AND ENVIRONMENT

It is no exaggeration to say that the Tibet I grew up in was a wildlife paradise. Animals were rarely hunted. Immense herds of *kyang* (wild asses) and *drong* (wild yak) roamed the plains along with shimmering *gowa* (gazelles), *wa* (fox), and *tsoe* (antelope). The noble eagles soared high over the monasteries and at night the call of the *wookpa* (long-eared owl) could be heard. Now, because of loss of habitat and hunting, the wildlife of my country is gone. In addition, Tibet's forests have been clear-cut by the Chinese, and Beijing admits that this is at least partly to blame for the catastrophic flooding in western China. Sensitivity to the environment must be part of realizing the universal dimensions of our actions, and restraint in this, as in all, is important.

ON NON-VIOLENCE

Chairman Mao once said political power comes from the barrel of a gun. But I believe that while violence may achieve short-term objectives, it cannot obtain long-lasting ends. I am a firm believer that violence begets violence. Some may say that my devotion to non-violence is praiseworthy, but not really practical. I am convinced people say that because engaging in it seems daunting and it is easy to become discouraged. But where once one only spoke of peace in one's land, now world peace is at stake—the fact of human interdependence is so explicit now. And we must recognize that non-violence was the principal characteristic of the political revolutions that swept the world during the 1980s. I have advanced the idea that Tibet, among other places, become a Zone of Peace, where countries like India and China, which have been at war for a long time, would benefit enormously from the establishment of a demilitarized area, saving a considerable portion of their income, which is presently wasted in maintaining border troops.

On a personal level, violence can undermine greater motivations. For example, I feel that hunger strikes as a vehicle of protest are problematic. The first time I visited the Tibetan hunger strikers (on April 2, 1988, in New Delhi), they had been without food for two weeks, so their physical condition was not yet too bad. Right from the beginning they asked me not to stop them. Since they undertook the hunger strike for the Tibetan issue, which is also my responsibility, in order to stop them I had to show them an alternative. But sadly there was no alternative. At last, Indian police intervened and took the strikers to the hospital, and I was immensely relieved. Yet the strikers acted with courage and determination, which is remarkable, and fortunately they did not have to die, not because they changed their minds, but because they were forced to live by the Indian government. The strikers did not consider self-sacrifice to be a form of violence, but I did. Although they realized that our cause was a just one, they should not have felt that death at the hands of the perceived enemy was a reasonable consequence for their actions. This is a distinction and an important one.

ON HUMAN RIGHTS

Human rights violations are symptoms of the larger issue of Tibet, and unless the world community tackles the Tibet issue, the human rights violations will continue. Meanwhile, the Tibetans suffer, the Chinese are embarrassed, and general resentment increases. The Chinese authorities are concerned about unity and stability, but their method of dealing with Tibet creates instability and disunity. It's a contradiction and does not work.

ON THE VALUE OF LIFE

I realize that being the Dalai Lama serves a purpose. If one's life becomes useful and beneficial for others, then its purpose is fulfilled. I have an immense responsibility and an impossible task. But as long as I carry on with sincere motivation, I become almost immune to these immense difficulties. Whatever I can do, I do; even if it is beyond my ability. Of course, I feel I would be more useful being outside government administration. Younger, trained people should do this, while my remaining time and energy should concentrate on the promotion of human value. Ultimately, that is the most important thing. When human value is not respected by those who administer governments or work on economic endeavors, then all sorts of problems, like crime and corruption, increase. The Communist ideology completely fails to promote human value, and corruption is consequently great. The Buddhist culture can help to increase self-discipline, and that will automatically reduce corruption. As soon as we can return to Tibet with a certain degree of freedom, I will hand over all my temporal authority. Then, for the rest of my life, I will focus on the promotion of human values and the promotion of harmony among the different religious traditions. I will continue teaching Buddhism to the Buddhist world.

ON GOALS AND IMPERMANENCE

There are no inherent contradictions between being a political leader and a moral leader, as long as you carry on political activities or goals with sincere motivation and proper goals. Proper goals mean not working for your own name, or for your own fame, or for your own power, but for the benefit of others.

Within another fifty years I, Tenzin Gyatso, will be no more than a memory. Time passes unhindered. The Chinese authorities and the Tibetan people very much want me to continue my work, but I am now over sixty-four years old. That means, in another ten years I will be seventy-four, in another twenty years I will be eighty-four. So, there is little time left for active work. My physicians say that my life span, as revealed by my pulse, is one hundred and three years. In this time, until my last day, I want to, for the benefit of all, maintain close relationships with those who became Tibet's friends during our darkest period. They did it not for money, certainly not for power (because by being our friends they may have had more inconvenience dealing with China), but out of human feeling, out of human concern. I consider these friendships very precious. Here is a short prayer that gave me great inspiration in my quest to benefit others:

> May I become at all times both now and forever
> A protector for those without protection
> A guide for those who have lost their way
> A ship for those with oceans to cross
> A bridge for those with rivers to cross
> A sanctuary for those in danger
> A lamp for those without light
> A place of rugs for those who lack shelter
> And a servant to all in need

CHINA, TIBET, AND A MESSAGE OF NON-VIOLENCE:
THE DALAI LAMA

HUMAN RIGHTS ISSUES: FREE EXPRESSION; RELIGIOUS FREEDOM

UNIVERSAL DECLARATION OF HUMAN RIGHTS:
Article: 18: Freedom of Belief and Religion

GUIDING QUESTION:
- What happens when you are not able to practice your religion?
- Why are groups denied the right to practice their religion? What role does religion play in the life of the individual, the community, a nation?

TIME REQUIREMENT:
Minimum 40 minutes, maximum 120 minutes

OBJECTIVES:
After this lesson, students will be able to:
- Understand the conflict between China and Tibet.
- Understand the concept of free expression/religious freedom and Article 18 from the Universal Declaration of Human Rights.
- Explain the Dalai Lama's message of non-violence and explore their own beliefs on non-violence as a solution to conflict.

VOCABULARY:
- Religious freedom
- Tibet
- China
- Non-violence
- Buddhism
- Compassion
- Intolerance

TECHNOLOGY REQUIRED:
- Internet access and computers for student research
- Interactive whiteboard if available (for presentations and viewing video) or LCD projector, computer, and screen

MATERIALS:
- Interview with the Dalai Lama
  www.rfkhumanrights.org / Click on Speak Truth To Power / click on "Curricula" link
- PBS *Speak Truth To Power* online passage on religious freedom and how it relates to Tibet:
  www.pbs.org/speaktruthtopower/issue_religious.html
- Video clip of the Dalai Lama talking about the situation in Tibet and his message of non-violence:
  video.nytimes.com/video/2009/05/28/world/1194840559273/an-interview-with-the-dalai-lama.html
- Article 18 from the Universal Declaration of Human Rights:
  www.un.org/en/documents/udhr/index.shtml#a18

STUDENT ACTIVITIES

ACTIVITY 1:
- Divide the students into small groups.
- Pass out the interview with the Dalai Lama.
- Assign students the reading on the Dalai Lama.
- Show students the video on the Dalai Lama.
- Ask each group to research and then craft a response to the interview and video following the guiding questions:
  - What is the main conflict between China and Tibet and how did it begin?
  - How does this conflict violate International Human Rights Law?
  - Who is the Dalai Lama?
- Explain his message on non-violence as a response to the conflict in Tibet.
- Instruct the students to include evidence from at least one source (other than the materials in class) to support their responses.
- Provide students a rubric to explain how the presentation will be evaluated.
- Group presentations may follow any of the below formats to convey their responses to the guiding questions:
  - Multimedia presentation PowerPoint, video, website, etc.
  - Group oral presentation
- Students must cite each source that they use in their presentation.
- After each group presents, it will field questions from the class on its presentation and provide a form for other students to evaluate its presentation.

CULMINATING ACTIVITY:
- Ask each student to select one key message from the interview with the Dalai Lama.
- Each student will complete the following writing assignment:

In 3-5 pages, answer the following questions:
  - How is the message you selected a global human rights issue? Please provide examples.
  - How can individuals play a role in bringing about change related to the key message you selected?

INTERNATIONAL HUMAN RIGHTS FRAMEWORK

Since the creation of the Universal Declaration of Human Rights (UDHR) by the United Nations (UN) in 1948, many other international documents have been drafted to develop these rights further. These documents include other declarations and resolutions, as well as treaties—which are also called covenants or conventions. Countries commit to protect the rights recognized in these documents. Sometimes a specific institution is created within the UN to monitor countries' compliance.

Here are examples of relevant international documents:

- International Covenant on Civil and Political Rights (ICCPR)
  - **Article 18:** Right to freedom of religion
  - **Article 24:** Protection of children without discrimination based on religion
  - **Article 26:** Prohibition of religious-based discrimination
  - **Article 27:** Right of minority communities to practice their own religion
- International Convention on the Elimination of All Forms of Racial Discrimination
- International Covenant on Economic, Social and Cultural Rights
- Declaration on the Elimination of All Forms of Intolerance and of Discrimination Based on Religion or Belief (1981)
- Declaration on the Rights of Persons Belonging to National or Ethnic Religious and Linguistic Minorities (1992)

For more information, visit the Office of the High Commissioner for Human Rights' website:
www.ohchr.org

BECOME A DEFENDER

The Dalai Lama often speaks about compassion for others and using non-violence as a way to respond to conflict. After reading about the events in Tibet, and learning about other regions in conflict across the globe, do you think non-violence can produce a positive outcome?

- On the personal level, think about the times you have been tempted to resolve a personal conflict by using some sort of violence and how that conflict could have been addressed in a non-violent manner. Also, think about how you can personally intervene in an escalating conflict between others using non-violent techniques.
- Pay attention to the news and pinpoint key stories in which non-violent methods have been used to resolve conflicts. The response can be in a format that the student decides is best to convey his or her response. For example, it could be a poem, short essay, art project, or video that is disseminated among classmates, the school and beyond.
- On the local level, are any efforts being carried out by the government, community groups or non-governmental organizations to resolve conflicts in your neighborhood or community? Interview people on all sides of the story; find out their thoughts the conflict and possible repercussions if the conflict is not resolved.
- On the national level and global level, ask yourself if your government is doing the best it can to help resolve violent or potentially violent conflicts around the world. Find out what independent agencies and advocacy groups are doing to help prevent or resolve a conflict. What is the media doing in your country to investigate and report areas of pending or ongoing conflict? If you believe that not enough is being done in your own country, contact the government entities responsible, advocacy groups or your government representative, congressperson or senator, to find out what is being done to resolve the pending or ongoing conflict peacefully. Contact them and either help to promote their work or criticize their work by writing to a newspaper. Discuss with your classmates some of the hot spots of conflict in the world and how these conflicts could be resolved by non-violent means.

"IF ONE'S LIFE BECOMES USEFUL AND BENEFICIAL FOR OTHERS, THEN ITS PURPOSE IS FULFILLED. I HAVE AN IMMENSE RESPONSIBILITY AND AN IMPOSSIBLE TASK. BUT AS LONG AS I CARRY ON WITH SINCERE MOTIVATION, I BECOME ALMOST IMMUNE TO THESE IMMENSE DIFFICULTIES. WHATEVER I CAN DO, I DO; EVEN IF IT IS BEYOND MY ABILITY. OF COURSE, I FEEL I WOULD BE MORE USEFUL BEING OUTSIDE GOVERNMENT ADMINISTRATION. YOUNGER, TRAINED PEOPLE SHOULD DO THIS, WHILE MY REMAINING TIME AND ENERGY SHOULD CONCENTRATE ON THE PROMOTION OF HUMAN VALUE. ULTIMATELY, THAT IS THE MOST IMPORTANT THING." –The Dalai Lama

ADDITIONAL RESOURCES

DALAI LAMA WEBSITE:
www.dalailama.com
The Dalai Lama's personal site, with numerous links to his teachings, messages and a wealth of video and audio from His Holiness.

CENTRAL TIBETAN ADMINISTRATION:
www.tibet.net/en/index.php
The official website of the current government of Tibet. It features information about current issues in Tibet and serves as a portal for news from other sources as well.

DALAI LAMA FOUNDATION:
www.dalailamafoundation.org/dlf/en/index.jsp
The Dalai Lama's personal foundation, established in 2002, that works to promote education about the importance of ethics and peace.

BACKGROUND ON THE DALAI LAMA:
www.lucidcafe.com/library/96jul/dalailama.html
A biography and set of resources about the Dalai Lama.

INTERNATIONAL CENTER ON NONVIOLENT CONFLICT:
www.nonviolent-conflict.org/
Extensive and frequently updated source for news about current and ongoing non-violent conflict and explanations of the concepts of non-violence.

MARTIN LUTHER KING, JR.'S 6 FACTS ABOUT NON-VIOLENT RESISTANCE:
www.care2.com/greenliving/martin-luther-king-six-facts.html
A good and simple introduction to non-violent resistance from one of its most famous proponents.

NONVIOLENCE INTERNATIONAL:
nonviolenceinternational.net
An NGO that focuses on promoting non-violence, with a great introduction to the principles of non-violence.

NON-VIOLENT STRUGGLE:
www.colorado.edu/conflict/peace/treatment/nonviolc.htm
Page from the University of Colorado website, with a great list of examples of non-violence.

UNITED STATES INSTITUTE OF PEACE:
www.usip.org
A U.S. government-funded institution with excellent resources for teaching peacemakers how to address conflict areas around the world.

"FEW MEN ARE WILLING TO BRAVE THE DISAPPROVAL OF THEIR FELLOWS, THE CENSURE OF THEIR COLLEAGUES, THE WRATH OF THEIR SOCIETY. MORAL COURAGE IS A RARER COMMODITY THAN BRAVERY IN BATTLE OR GREAT INTELLIGENCE. YET IT IS THE ONE ESSENTIAL, VITAL QUALITY FOR THOSE WHO SEEK TO CHANGE A WORLD WHICH YIELDS MOST PAINFULLY TO CHANGE."

—Robert F. Kennedy

JULIANA DOGBADZI
Ghana – Modern Slavery/Trafficking

Enslaved in a shrine in her native Ghana as a young child under a custom known as *Trokosi*, Juliana Dogbadzi was forced to work without pay, food, or clothing, and to perform sexual services for the holy man. She was able to escape seventeen years later, after several failed attempts, at the age of twenty-three. *Trokosi* comes from an Ewe word meaning "slave of the gods," and is understood as a religious and cultural practice in which young girls, mostly virgins, are sent into lifelong servitude to atone for the alleged crimes of their relatives. In 1997, it was estimated that approximately five thousand young girls and women were being kept in 345 shrines in the southeastern part of Ghana. Through Juliana Dogbadzi's daring escape and her subsequent efforts to denounce the system, the Trokosi practice was banned in Ghana in 1999; however, law enforcement against Trokosi is still lax. Dogbadzi continues to speak out against Trokosi, traveling the country, meeting with slaves, and trying to win their emancipation; increasingly, she is not alone in her courageous stance.

INTERVIEW TAKEN FROM KERRY KENNEDY'S BOOK *SPEAK TRUTH TO POWER*, 2000

"THERE ARE MORE WOMEN WHO REMAIN IN THE SHRINE WHO NEED HELP. NO ONE IS GOING TO REPRESENT THEM BETTER THAN SOMEONE WHO HAS BEEN IN THE SHRINE AND WHO HAS GONE THROUGH THE PAIN…AGAINST ALL ODDS, I DECIDED TO TAKE THE RESPONSIBILITY OF ADDRESSING THE ISSUE AND HAVE BEEN DOING SO EVER SINCE."–Juliana Dogbadzi

I have never been in a classroom. I have never been to school. When I was seven years old, my parents took me from our home and sent me to a shrine where I was a slave to a fetish priest for seventeen years. My grandfather, they said, had stolen two dollars. When he was suspected of the crime and asked to return the money, he defended his innocence. The woman who had accused him of the crime went to the shrine and cursed my grandfather's family, at which point members of my family began to die. In order to stop the deaths, a soothsayer told us that my grandfather would have to report to the Trokosi shrine. The priest told my family that it must bring a young girl to the shrine to appease the gods. A sister was sent to the shrine at Kebenu some six hundred miles away, but she died a few years later. Since I had been born just after my grandfather's death, I became her replacement.

I lived and worked in the priest's fields and kept the compound clean. While doing so, I was raped repeatedly by the priest on torn mats on the cold floor of windowless huts. The other female slaves and I received neither food nor medical care. We had to find time after working on the priest's farm to burn charcoal or to sell firewood in the nearest town in order to make enough money to buy food. There were times we lived on raw peppers or palm kernel nuts to stay alive.

Because I was just a kid, I didn't know what to do. There was an elder woman who was a slave and took care of me. She couldn't help me much because she had so many kids as a consequence of being raped by the priest. She said, "Look, little girl, take care of yourself or you will die." There used to be a hundred women slaves in my shrine, but the priest sent about ninety of them to work on his farms in other villages. Collectively, they had about sixty-five children and would have to work to look after the children.

Twelve of us, four women and eight children, lived in a one-room, thatched-roof house. It was built of mud and lacked both windows and doors. The rain got in. The snakes got in. The room was twenty feet long and twelve feet wide. The ceiling was low, just shy of our heads, and we all slept together on a mat on the floor. This is not everything that I can remember, but saying it brings back pains of old and it's difficult to go back through all those experiences.

You see, in the shrine you have no right to put on shoes or a hat to protect yourself against the hot sun. If it is raining or cold, you have only a small piece of cloth around yourself. A typical day in the shrine was as follows: you wake up at five o'clock in the morning, go to the stream about five kilometers away to get water for the compound, sweep, prepare meals for the priest (not eating any yourself), go to the farm, work until six o'clock, and return to sleep without food or to scrounge for leftovers. At night, the priest would call one of us to his room and would rape us. I was about twelve when I was first raped.

There was favoritism even in slavery. The priest liked girls who would readily give in to his sexual demands and hated those who would always put up a fight. Consequently, these girls were beaten. The ones he liked always said they were being wise because they wanted to avoid being beaten, while some of us maintained that they were foolish and were enjoying sex with a man they didn't love. When I saw people who came to the village to buy food wearing nice dresses, I started to think that I had to do something for myself. I had to get freedom.

I had to do something that would change my life. I escaped several times. The first time I escaped, I went to my parents. I told them I was suffering in the shrine, but they were scared to keep me. They said that if they did, the gods would strike them dead.

They brought me back to the priest to suffer the same pain again. I thought, no. This is not going to happen again. I had to find a way to free myself and free the other women, too.

The second time I escaped, I went to a nearby village. A young man fed me and took me to himself. He took advantage of me and made me pregnant. When the priest found out, he sent young men around the village to get me. They beat me endlessly and I had lots of cuts on my body. I collapsed and nearly died. The child's father had wanted to take care of us, but the priest threatened him with death. The young man who was taking care of me was asked to pay some bottles of hard liquor and a fowl and warned to stay away from me or die. I haven't seen him since and he hasn't seen our child.

The third time I escaped, I resolved that I would never again go back to the shrine. By this time, I was three months pregnant as a result of another rape that I had suffered from the priest. I was not feeling very well. For a number of days I had starved. I was pregnant and needed to get some food. Otherwise, I was going to die. I decided to go to a nearby farm owned by the priest to get an ear of corn from the crop which the other slaves in the shrine and I had planted. I was caught stealing the corn and the priest ordered the young men around the village to beat me until I fell unconscious. When I came to, I saw all the bruises and wounds on my body and nearly lost the baby I was carrying. I decided I had to leave or I would be killed. But it was not to be. I was scared and I went back to the shrine again. Yet, that was the turning point. I was about seventeen or eighteen at the time and resolved that I was going to do something to help other people in the shrine.

One day, a man representing a nonprofit organization called International Needs–Ghana came to the shrine to talk to the priest. This was my chance. I don't know where my sudden confidence came from, but all my fear had disappeared. I was no longer afraid of death and was prepared to die for others. Thank God I had that feeling! I did not escape immediately because I was very weak, my pregnancy was well advanced and I could not walk a long distance. Luckily, I had the baby a few weeks later. With the baby strapped to my back and the first child, Wonder, in my hands, I escaped through the bush to the major street where I was given a lift to Adidome and to the site of International Needs–Ghana.

The members of the organization taught me a lot of skills and kept me away from the priest. They trained me in bread baking and other vocations. Nonetheless, I thought, "There are more women who remain in the shrine who need help. No one is going to represent them better than someone who has been in the shrine and who has gone through the pain, someone who can tell the world what happens in the shrine. If no one stops this practice, we will all have to die in pain." Against all odds, I decided to take the responsibility of addressing the issue and have been doing so ever since. I went to the shrines and spoke to the inmates. I told them that they needed to gather courage like I had and to get out.

The shrine claims powers it does not have in order to instill fear in the slaves and to stop them from escaping. The practice is a deliberate attempt by men to subjugate women. A man commits a crime and a woman has to pay for it. That is unacceptable. Likewise, the shrine is a crime against children. The child of a slave shares his mother's plight. When the mother has food to eat, the child eats. If she has no food, the child will starve. If she has clothing, the child will likewise have some. If not, that is it. If she goes to the farm, the child goes along. There are thousands of women Trokosi slaves with children who need to be helped. Those who have been liberated also require help in order to recover from the suffering endured in the shrines.

Unlike most of the other girls and women, I got over the fear instilled by the Trokosi system. This was my weapon. Now that I have escaped, I help to diminish the women's fears by telling them my story. I tell them what I am presently doing, that I am still alive, not dead, as they have been made to believe. I try to help the priests to understand the pain that the women have endured. Some do not allow me to enter their shrines any longer. When I am in the city, I educate people about life in the shrines and advocate for an end to the practice.

What I do is dangerous, but I am prepared to die for a good cause. People send threats by letter and others confront me openly. Thank God that those I work with are very strong and give me encouragement. At the moment, eight girls have joined me in my work with the organization. My next step to disbanding Trokosi is to ensure enforcement of the law and to get allied organizations in the Republics of Togo and Benin to stop this practice in their respective countries.

I do believe I have a calling because it is strange to be alive and sane and working after going through what I went through. The help that I have received from International Needs and my own confidence have made all the difference. I have totally forgiven my parents because I know that what they did to me was done through ignorance and fear. I don't want them to feel guilty so I avoid telling them about my experiences. I don't, however, see them often. I am glad to say that I am now happily married and have just had my first planned baby with the man I love. My life today is like the life of any other young woman.

DEFENDER AGAINST MODERN SLAVERY AND TRAFFICKING
JULIANA DOGBADZI

HUMAN RIGHTS ISSUE: MODERN SLAVERY/TRAFFICKING

UNIVERSAL DECLARATION OF HUMAN RIGHTS:
- **Article 1:** Right to Equality
- **Article 2:** Freedom from Discrimination
- **Article 3:** Right to Life, Liberty, and Personal Security
- **Article 4:** Freedom from Slavery
- **Article 5:** Freedom from Torture and Degrading Treatment
- **Article 6:** Right to Recognition as a Person before the Law
- **Article 7:** Right to Equality before the Law

GUIDING QUESTIONS:
- If slavery is illegal, why does it exist throughout the world today?
- For what reasons do governments turn a blind eye to human trafficking and slavery?
- How can effective change occur?

TIME REQUIREMENT:
40 minutes

OBJECTIVES:
After this lesson, students will be able to:
- Recognize the issue of human trafficking and its relationship to modern slavery.
- Listen to an excerpt about Juliana Dogbadzi and discuss the source of her enslavement, the results of her enslavement, and the ultimate outcome of her situation.
- Reflect on the concept of paying for the wrongs of another person in order to recognize the ways in which the issue relates to their own lives.
- Brainstorm ideas for taking action against these violations of human rights.
- Write for personal reflection to assess their understanding of the issue.
- Propose and implement an action.

VOCABULARY:
- Trafficking
- Trokosi
- Shrine
- Fetish Priest
- Non-governmental organizations
- Advocate
- Trafficking Victims' Protection Act

CONCEPTS:
- Human trafficking
- Sex slavery
- Fear
- Subjugation
- Advocacy

TEACHER TIP:
Both vocabulary and concepts must be taught prior to the lesson.

TECHNOLOGY REQUIRED:
- Internet access with YouTube available
- Projector from the computer to screen or interactive whiteboard
- Student Response System, if possible

MATERIALS:
- Index cards
- Glossary of relevant terms
  www.wgbh.org/articles/Human-Trafficking-Glossary-of-Terms-289
- Discussion questions
  blogs.nysut.org/sttp/2010/11/09/juliana-dogbadzi-slaverytrafficking/
- YouTube video on modern slavery:
  www.YouTube.com/watch?v=HRwaM9lCRrM
- Dogbadzi bio and interview:
  www.rfkhumanrights.org / click on Speak Truth To Power / click on "Curricula" link

STUDENT ACTIVITIES

ANTICIPATORY SET:
- Ask students to consider the following questions and poll their answers:
  - Is slavery legal anywhere in the world today?
  - If slavery exists today, how many slaves do you think there are?
  - Do you think the number is greater than, less than, or equal to the number of slaves in America at the time of emancipation? Are there slaves in America today?
- Show the YouTube video on modern slavery and refer to previous questions for a class discussion after viewing:
  www.youtube.com/watch?v=HRwaM9lCRrM.

TEACHER TIP: Post the four questions on the board and ask students to consider them prior to the bell. (Bell Ringer Activity)

ACTIVITY 1:
- Provide a brief background about Juliana Dogbadzi. Read the excerpt from *Speak Truth To Power* to the class, having the students take notes on the handout with questions for discussion: blogs.nysut.org/sttp/2010/11/09/juliana-dogbadzi-slaverytrafficking/
- Distribute the questions for discussion.
- After reading is completed, provide time for discussion in response to the questions.

ACTIVITY 2:
- Brainstorm ways in which students can take action and become defenders.

BECOME A DEFENDER

Students will select one of the following projects to advocate for the end of slavery:
- Research what the United States Department of State is doing currently to stop human trafficking and write an article for the school newsletter or the local newspaper about the problem and ways in which it can be addressed.
- Research the efforts being made by a specific NGO to stop trafficking and write an article about its efforts for the school newsletter.
- Make a video highlighting the injustices of human trafficking that can be shown to the student body.
- Create and publish a glog that provides text, audio, and media to expose the issue and raise awareness (www.edu.glogster.com). Teachers can get free accounts for their students by registering at the glogster site.
- Write a letter to your Senator or Representative expressing your concerns about the lack of enforcement of the Universal Declaration of Human Rights and request his or her intervention.
- Contact an NGO that fights against trafficking and arrange for a speaker to come to your class, school, or a community event in order to raise awareness.
- Start a fund drive to contribute to an NGO that works toward ending human trafficking.

TEACHER TIP: The lesson can be easily expanded into more than one 40-minute period. If discussion time is needed, expansion is highly recommended. Additional resources will enable teachers and students to learn more about the extensive problem of human trafficking and slavery in today's world, either together or independently.

INTERNATIONAL HUMAN RIGHTS FRAMEWORK

Since the creation of the Universal Declaration of Human Rights (UDHR) by the United Nations (UN) in 1948, many other international documents have been drafted to develop these rights further. These documents include other declarations and resolutions, as well as treaties—which are also called covenants or conventions. Countries commit to protect the rights recognized in these documents. Sometimes a specific institution is created within the UN to monitor countries' compliance.

Here are examples of relevant international documents:

- Convention Against Torture and Other Cruel, Inhuman or Degrading Treatment or Punishment
   - Article 1: definition of torture and CIDT
   - Article 4: obligation to penalize acts of torture
- International Covenant on Civil and Political Rights
- Convention on the Elimination of All Forms of Discrimination Against Women
- Convention on the Rights of the Child

For more information, visit the Office of the High Commissioner for Human Rights' website:
www.ohchr.org

ADDITIONAL RESOURCES

FREETHESLAVES.NET:
www.freetheslaves.net
This site includes a variety of information about human trafficking and finding a solution to end slavery in our time.

TRAFFICKING IN PERSONS REPORT 2010:
www.state.gov/g/tip/rls/tiprpt/2010/index.htm
Excellent source of current information about human trafficking, including: an interactive map; narratives on each country discussing the level of their involvement, their efforts to eradicate the problem, and the recommendations to increase effectiveness of efforts; victims' stories; and many other resources.

POLARIS PROJECT:
www.polarisproject.org/
Another rich source from an NGO. Included are survivor stories, current actions, ways to get involved, etc.

PBS FRONTLINE:
www.pbs.org/wgbh/pages/frontline/slaves/etc/stats.html
A resource with valuable links to NGOs and many articles.

PBS FRONTLINE MODERN SLAVERY DOCUMENTARY:
freedocumentaries.org/film.php?id=161
Includes a free download of Frontline's documentary about sex slavery. There are also links to two other documentaries on modern slavery.

PBS FRONTLINE MAP:
www.pbs.org/wgbh/pages/frontline/slaves/map/indexflash.html
This link takes you to a PBS–Frontline interactive map that accompanies the story on sex slaves.

THE TROKOSI IN GHANA:
www.sos-sexisme.org/English/slavery.htm
Article on the Trokosi in Ghana.

INTERNATIONAL NEEDS TRANSFORMING THE LIVES OF WOMEN IN GHANA:
www.internationalneeds.org.au/Ghana
Extensive information on the Trokosi in Ghana and the work this NGO is doing to end the practice.

GHANA'S SLAVES TO THE GODS:
www.wcl.american.edu/hrbrief/v7i1/ghana.htm
A powerful article about the practice in Ghana and Juliana Dogbadzi.

21ST CENTURY SLAVES:
ngm.nationalgeographic.com/ngm/0309/feature1/
National Geographic—info and multiple links to resources.

SPEAK TRUTH TO POWER: VOICES FROM BEYOND THE DARK

A play by Ariel Dorfman
Adapted from *Speak Truth To Power*, a book by Kerry Kennedy

A MESSAGE FROM THE PLAYWRIGHT

It has not been easy for these voices to reach us. First, they had to overcome fear. There is always fear at the beginning of every voyage, fear and its malignant twin, violence, at the beginning of every voyage into courage.

The bodies that housed these voices either suffered that violence personally or they witnessed that violence being visited upon another human being, a group, a nation. Some saw a father or a son or a wife abducted in the night and taken away. Others saw children made into warriors and forced to kill at an early age. Each one of them saw something intolerable: a man killed because of the color of his skin or the color of his opinions, people taken into airless chambers and executed in cold blood, soldiers turning their guns against the people, women hated because of their sexual choices. They saw ancestral lands being stolen from their owners, forests devastated, languages forbidden. They saw books censored, friends subjected to torture, youngsters made into slaves. They saw lawyers jailed and exiled because they defended the victims.

And then something happened. Something extraordinary and almost miraculous. They found a way of speaking out, decided that they could not live with themselves if they did nothing, they could not stain their lives by remaining silent. And as they spoke out, they discovered that not the violence, but the fear, slowly disappeared. When they spoke out and found others on the road with them, other voices, from near and far, they began to find ways of controlling that fear instead of letting the fear control them.

I had been preparing all my life for the chance to become a bridge for them. Ever since I was a child and was moved by the injustices I saw around me, and then as an adolescent, as I realized that those outrages existed in far more grievous forms beyond my immediate horizon. Then as a young man when it was my turn to see a dictatorship take over my country, Chile, and watch my friends persecuted and murdered while I was spared, when it became my turn to go into exile and wander the globe and everywhere remark the same inequities mirrored in land after land, when it became my turn to try and figure out how I could write stories and find the words that explored the vast heart of human suffering and the vaster complexity and enigmas of evil, ever since then I had been waiting for the occasion to put my art yet one more time at the service of those who had kept me warm in the midst of my own struggles.

And I have been fortunate enough to have received those voices like you receive a blessing in the dark and to have given them a dramatic form. It took me my whole life to find a voice of my own to accompany these voices.

Take the voices home with you, carry them into the world. It is a world that needs changing. Knowing this, knowing this: the world does not have to forever be the way it is now.

ARIEL DORFMAN, the Chilean-American writer and human rights activist, is a distinguished professor at Duke University and has written books in Spanish and English that have been translated into more than 40 languages. His plays have been staged in more than 100 countries and have received numerous awards, including the Laurence Olivier Award (for "Death and the Maiden," which was made into a feature film by Roman Polanski). Dorfman's most recent play premieres include "The Other Side" in Tokyo, Japan in 2004, "Purgatorio" in Seattle in 2005, "Picasso's Closet" in Washington, D.C. in 2006, and his musical, "Dancing Shadows" in Seoul, South Korea in 2007. He is also the subject of a feature-length documentary, *A Promise to the Dead,* based on his memoir *Heading South, Looking North,* directed by Peter Raymont, which premiered at the 2007 Toronto International Film Festival. In July 2010 he delivered the Nelson Mandela Lecture in South Africa.

Excerpts based on Ariel Dorfman's play
"SPEAK TRUTH TO POWER: VOICES FROM BEYOND THE DARK"

LIGHTS RISE ON THE EIGHT ACTORS, FOUR MEN, FOUR WOMEN, GROUPED SYMMETRICALLY.

FIRST VOICE (MALE)
Courage begins with one voice.
It's that simple.
I did what I had to do.
That is what we know.
You walk into the corridor of death and you know.

LIGHTS RISE ON THE MAN AND WOMAN, TO ONE SIDE, SEPARATE FROM THE DEFENDERS.

MAN
They know. They can't say they don't know.

WOMAN
They can't say they don't walk into this with their eyes open.

FIRST VOICE (MALE)
You walk into the corridor of death and you know.
You know this moment might be your last.

SECOND VOICE (FEMALE)
You walk into the corridor of death. . .

FIRST VOICE (MALE)
. . . and you know, you know this moment might be your last.

SECOND VOICE (FEMALE)
That is what you know.

THIRD VOICE (FEMALE)
I know what it is to wait in the dark for torture and what it is to wait in the dark for truth.
I did what I had to do.
Anything else would have tasted like ashes.

WOMAN
They can't say they don't know.

SECOND VOICE (FEMALE)
My name is Malala Yousafzai.

WOMAN MAKES A GESTURE AND THE NAME (OR IMAGE OF) MALALA YOUSAFZAI APPEARS ON THE SCREEN.

In January, 2009, when I was in 7th grade, I started blogging for the BBC about a Taliban edict in Pakistan's Swat Valley that banned girls like me from going to school. I wanted to scream, shout, and tell the whole world what we were going through. But it was not possible. The Taliban would have killed me, my father, my whole family. So I chose to write with a different name. And it worked. My valley has been freed.

Still, I paid a price. On October 9th, 2012, the Taliban shot me on the left side of my forehead as I rode the bus home from school. They shot my friends, too. They thought that the bullets would silence us. But they failed. Suddenly, the few of us calling for justice in Pakistan were joined by thousands of voices around the world.

The terrorists thought that they would change our aims and crush our ambitions, but nothing changed in my life except this: weakness, fear, and hopelessness died. My courage is as strong as ever. I am the same Malala. My ambitions are the same. My hopes are the same. My dreams are the same. Speak Truth To Power.

WOMAN
And this is what they really fear: that nobody cares, that people forget, that people watch t.v. and say these are not their problems and then have dinner and then go to sleep. People go to sleep.

MAN
People go to sleep. That is what they know and fear. They know that three billion people live in poverty and forty thousand children die each day of diseases that could be prevented.

WOMAN
They know that the three richest people in the world. . .

MAN
. . . have assets that exceed the combined gross domestic product of the poorest forty eight countries. And that is not going to change by saving one life and then another and then another. Nothing is ever going to change. This is what they fear: that nobody really cares.

FIRST VOICE (MALE)
My name is Oscar Arias Sánchez. And I care.

WOMAN MAKES A GESTURE AND THE NAME (OR IMAGE OF) OSCAR ARIAS SÁNCHEZ APPEARS ON THE SCREEN.

Military spending is not merely a consumer excess; instead it represents a huge perversion in the priorities of our civilization: 780 billion dollars each year invested in instruments of death, in guns and fighters designed to kill people that could be spent on human development. If we channeled just five per cent of that figure over the next ten years, just five per cent of those billions, into anti-poverty programs, all of the world's population would enjoy basic social services. The poor of the world are crying out for schools and doctors, not guns and generals.

MAN
Yes. Of course the poor of the world are crying out. But who cares?

FOURTH VOICE (MALE)
My name is Jamie Nabozy.

MAN MAKES A GESTURE AND THE NAME (OR IMAGE OF) JAMIE NABOZNY APPEARS ON THE SCREEN.

When I was in seventh grade, Kids were calling me 'fag' and 'queer'. I told the guidance counselor who directed me to the Principal of the school. And the Principal said 'I'll take care of it', but nothing changed.

One day I was in a bathroom with my brother and some kids actually ended up pushing us into the stalls and punching us. And I thought, "Okay, now that it's turned violent the Principal has to do something." But she said to me, "Jamie, if you're going to be so openly gay, these kinds of things are going to happen to you."

I attempted to kill myself.

Partially through my eighth grade year I was in science class, and two boys started groping me and grabbing me and pushed me to the ground and pretended like they were raping me in front of the entire class. I ran to the Principal's office, expecting, surely, she's going to do something now, it's a sexual thing. And she just looked at me and shook her head and said, "Jamie, if you don't have an appointment then I don't have anything to say to you."

In high school, they beat me so badly I had to be taken to the hospital; I had to have emergency abdominal surgery for internal bruising and bleeding. I knew I wasn't ever going to be safe at school.

Then I met this crazy lesbian lawyer and we won. And school administrators now have a personal responsibility to protect students from harassment and if they do not they can be individually be sued, like a doctor for malpractice. I've always said I don't care why people do the right thing; they just need to do the right thing.

Speak Truth To Power.

Visit www.rfkhumanrights.org *for the full-length play and additional Defender monologues*

ACKNOWLEDGEMENTS

Speak Truth To Power was created with the help of many. I am most grateful to all the defenders who took the time to participate in this project, for sharing their lives, their time, their innermost thoughts. What started out as a survey became, ultimately, a spiritual journey about the power of one.

This book, and the original book, were a collaborative effort. I want to thank Eddie Adams for all the time, effort, and energy he devoted to this project, and for going forward when the going got rough. Eddie was a dear friend, an amazing photographer, and a blessing to all who knew him. He passed away in 2004, but his photographs live on as a lasting tribute to his genius. In this edition, other photographers contributed work, including George Ballis/ The Stock/ The Image Word, Andrea Erikson/ Andrea Joan Photography, Olivia Harris/Corbis, Bob Lerner, Anders Pettersson, Jeffry Salter, Maggie Stebber and Lonnie Tague.

In the theater presentation, thanks first to Ariel Dorfman for his superlative efforts in making a true drama out of these interviews, and his energetic work over the last two decades and more in supporting the play in dozens of countries. Thank you to President Clinton for hosting the play when it opened at the John F. Kennedy Center for the Performing arts, and our first cast— John Malkovich, Kevin Kline, Sigourney Weaver, Alfre Woodard, Rita Moreno, Hector Elizondo, Alec Baldwin, Giancarlo Esposito and Julia Louis Dreyfus. Thank you to Marco Alemanno, Harry Belafonte, Alexis Bledel, Elena Bouryka, Lorraine Bracco, Anna Buonaiuto, Mimmo Calopresti, Aldo Cazzullo, Michela Cescon, Glenn Close, Lucio Dalla, Piera Degli Esposti, Trevor Donovan, Niccolo Fabi, America Ferrera, Beppe Fiorello, Anna Galiena, Marcia Gay Harden, Andrea Giordana, Rupert Graves, Charles Grodin, Alessandro Haber, Woody Harrelson, Dennis Haysbert, Bob Herbert, Enzo Iacchetti, Laura Innes, Saeed Jaffrey, Catherine Keener, Richard Kind, Gad Lerner, Enrico Lo Verso, Tiziana Lodato, Fiorella Mannoia, Julianna Margulies, Pietro Mazzarella, Matthew Modine, Alfred Molina, Julianne Moore, Viggo Mortensen, Bill Nighy, Lena Olin, Silvio Orlando, Julia Ormond, Mandy Patinkin, Matthew Morrison, Sean Penn, Michele Placido, Maria Rondanini, Lynn Redgrave, Vanessa Redgrave, Gloria Reuben, Lina Sastri, Michele Serra, Rufus Sewell, Vittorio Sgarbi, Martin Sheen, Christian Slater, Kevin Sorbo, Paul Sorvino, Juliet Stevenson, Sharon Stone, Meryl Streep, Janet Suzman, Oliviero Toscani, Stanley Tucci, Ornella Vanoni, Sam Waterston, Bradley Whitford, Debra Winger and Robin Wright, and many others, who were so generous with their time and talent.

Over the course of the years since Crown Books/ Random House first published the first edition, the project has grown exponentially. A special thanks to Speak Truth To Power, Executive Director John Heffernan, for his unsurpassed leadership and vision. The Speak Truth To Power human rights curriculum is now being taught to millions of students around the world in such places as Cambodia, Canada, France, Greece, Italy, Hong Kong, Nicaragua, Norway, Portugal, Romania, Rwanda, South Africa, Spain, Sweden, Switzerland, and the United States. This could not be possible without Speak Truth To Power staff including Karen Robinson, Jenny Girardi, and Mary McCoy, and our incredible volunteers from around the world.

A very special thanks to Robert Smith for his unwavering support of the Robert F. Kennedy Human Rights, our founder Mrs. Robert F. Kennedy and to our entire Board of Directors, Frank Baker, Peter Barbey, Harry Belafonte, Alan H. Buerger, Tim Cook, Larry Cox, Peter Edelman, Mark E. Freitas, Jonah Goodhart, Claudio Grossman, Richard Iannuzzi, Philip W. Johnston, Joseph P. Kennedy III, Matthew Kennedy, Niclas Kjellström-Matseke, Marialina Marcucci, Elisa Massimino, Terry Mazany, James J. Pinto, Michael Posner, John Rogers, Marvin S. Rosen, Malika Saada Saar, Dr. Jeffrey Sachs, Henry D. Schleiff, Martin Sheen, Donato Tramuto, Luz Vega-Marquis, Paul Van Zyl, Anthony Williams, and Robert Wolf.

Writing this incomplete acknowledgment makes me realize how blessed I am to be involved in human rights, in work so compelling that it naturally creates an expansive support network. We are not alone. Thanks to you all.

Albert Camus said, "In the depth of winter, I finally learned that within me, there lay an invincible summer." My love to my three girls who never fail to remind me of all the joys of summer, without and within: Cara, Mariah and Michaela.

Kerry Kennedy, 2016

Copyright © 2016 by Kerry Kennedy
Photographs copyright © 2016 by Eddie Adams
Other Photography:
- Page 14: © Lonnie Tague
- Page 37: © George Ballis/Take Stock/The Image Works
- Page 42: © Maggie Steber
- Page 46: © Jeffery Salter
- Page 57: © Bob Lerner
- Page 58: © Olivia Harris/Corbis
- Page 66: © Andrea Erickson/Andrea Joan Photography
- Page 85: Courtesy of JFK Library
- Page 86: © Anders Pettersson/Getty Images

All rights reserved.

Published by Robert F. Kennedy Human Rights

ISBN 978-0-692-77495-3

Editors: Kerry Kennedy, President, Robert F. Kennedy Human Rights
Book Design: Jennifer Kakaletris Design LLC

Please visit our website at: www.rfkhumanrights.org
@RFKHumanRights
RFKHumanRights

Printed in the United States of America through
Four Colour Print Group, Louisville, Kentucky